GOOD HOME
HOUSEKEEPING BAKING

GOOD HOUSEKEEPING

by Good Housekeeping Institute

BOOK CLUB

HOME BAKING

Illustrated by Hilary Evans

ASSOCIATES
London

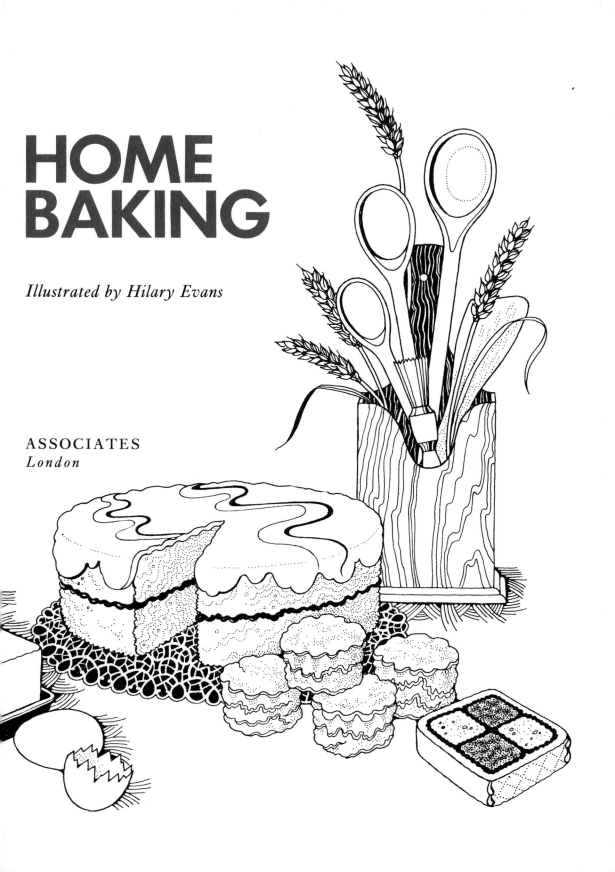

This edition published 1977 by
Book Club Associates
by arrangement with
Ebury Press

Editor Amanda Atha
Home economist Mary Walker
Designer Derek Morrison

Colour plates and jacket by Melvin Grey

Filmset and printed in Great Britain by
BAS Printers Ltd, Wallop, Hampshire
and bound by
Hazell Watson and Viney Ltd
Aylesbury, Bucks

Contents

Colour Plates

Foreword

We get more queries about home baking than anything else at Good Housekeeping. Perhaps this is because the British housewife's cookery skill is judged by the quality of her baking. 'If I'd known you were coming I'd have baked a cake' is our natural reaction when we want to please a friend. In contrast, the French or German housewife will run to the patisserie and buy a creamy confection. However, in spite of our love of home baking some people understandably lack the confidence to tackle anything more complicated than scones, Victoria sandwiches and straightforward bread. Baking needs precision to get perfect, consistent results. Weighing the ingredients accurately is important, so is choosing the right size of tin and using the correct oven temperature.

All the recipes in this book have been double tested in the famous Good Housekeeping Institute kitchens and we are confident that if you follow them precisely you'll get good results. You'll be able to perfect your breadmaking and try your hand at Sally Lunns and croissants as well. You'll be able to increase your repertoire of family cakes and cookies and even make some mouthwatering gâteaux, such as Black Forest cake or Orange liqueur gâteau. Blow the calories, we're not going to be weaned from our baps, brioches and Dundee cakes!

If you have any problems with any of these recipes just write to the address below enclosing a stamped addressed envelope and we shall be pleased to do all we can to help.

CAROL MACARTNEY

Director

Good Housekeeping Institute
Chestergate House
Vauxhall Bridge Road
London SW1V 1HF

Basic Breadmaking

Nothing is more evocative than the smell of new baked bread filling every corner of the kitchen. More has been written in its praise than on almost any other subject. Bread has a long and fascinating history, going right back to the Neolithic age. Tombs of the Pharaohs have pictures showing what is thought to be the fermenting of yeast (a process they probably discovered). Little has changed in the actual processes involved in bread making – though the housewife of the middle ages might have had to mill her corn before starting on the dough – but each country has evolved its own version of the daily bread, based on local corn crops. Flat, unleavened bread of barley, millet, maize or buckwheat belongs to Asia and Africa; the traditional Latin American tortillas are made of maize. Rye breads are popular in Germany, Scandinavia and Russia. Here and in the United States we favour wheat.

Something we tend to forget is that bread is good for you. It is rich in vitamins (particularly the B group) calcium, iron and trace elements. Bran (in wholemeal flour) provides the roughage essential to high fibre diets. And – surprise to slimmers! – bread has only five more calories per ounce than lean beef and is a useful source of protein. What more could anyone want?

The ingredient which gives bread its mouth-watering characteristic smell is yeast, the oldest and for centuries the only form of raising agent. You will find it quite easy to use once you realise it is a living plant and, like most plants, requires gentle warmth, food and water in order to grow. These last two requirements are usually supplied by the carbohydrate in flour and the liquid used in making dough. With their help and with warmth, the yeast grows rapidly and, again like all living plants, 'breathes' out a harmless gas – carbon dioxide. It is the expansion of this gas that makes the dough rise and gives it an open texture. Too much heat kills the yeast altogether; too little retards its growth – so read the step by step instructions on dough making to make quite sure you know what's what before you start cooking with yeast.

Ingredients used in breadmaking

Yeast

You can now buy fresh yeast from health stores and some bakers (those who bake their own bread are your best bet) and dried yeast can be found in chemists, supermarkets and grocers as well as health food stores. Which is best, dried or fresh? Both have their pros and cons as explained below. There is nothing to choose between the two as far as taste and texture of the end result is concerned.

Fresh yeast is rather like putty in colour and texture and should have a faint 'winey' smell. There should be no discoloration and it should crumble easily when broken. Although it will store for up to a month in a screw-topped jar or wrapped in cling film or foil in the refrigerator, the best results are obtained when it is absolutely fresh, so buy it in small quantities when required.

Fresh yeast is usually blended with a liquid (*see page 13*), it is then ready to be added to the flour all at once. It can also be rubbed directly into the flour or else added as a batter. This batter is known as the sponge dough process where only some of the ingredients are mixed, forming a sponge that is allowed to ferment and is then mixed with the remaining ingredients to form a dough.

Using sugar to cream the yeast before adding the liquid is not advised as sugar kills some of the yeast cells and delays fermentation. The resulting bread has a strong yeasty taste. Fresh yeast is easiest measured by weight. According to the richness of the mixture, 25 g (1 oz) fresh yeast is sufficient to raise 1.4 kg (3 lb) white flour.

Dried yeast is sold in granulated form and is very convenient as it can be stored in an airtight container in a cool place for up to six months. Take care when buying it that it is bakers' yeast and not tonic or brewers' yeast as these have no rising powers. Dried yeast requires sugar and liquid to activate it. The sugar, in the proportion of 5 ml (1 level tsp) to 300 ml ($\frac{1}{2}$ pint) of tepid liquid, is dissolved in the liquid. The yeast granules are then sprinkled over the surface of the liquid and the mixture left to froth for about 15 minutes before being ready for use. Dried yeast is easiest measured in 5 ml (1 tsp) or 15 ml (1 tbsp) spoonfuls. As it is more concentrated than fresh yeast, generally half the amount of dried yeast is required to fresh yeast. 15 ml (1 level tbsp) dried yeast is equivalent to 25 g (1 oz) fresh yeast.

To avoid repetition of instructions yeast recipes have been written using fresh yeast, but dried yeast can be used equally successfully.

Flour

Wheat, before it is made into flour, is either hard or soft. Hard wheat when milled produces a strong flour, rich in protein, which contains a sticky, rubber-like substance called gluten. When combined with the other essential ingredients used in breadmaking, the gluten stretches like elastic and as it is heated, it expands and traps in the dough the carbon dioxide released by the yeast. The gluten then sets and forms the 'frame' of the bread. A strong plain flour should have a gluten content of 10–15 per cent. It is the gluten content in a strong flour that gives the volume and open texture of baked bread.

Soft wheats when milled produce a flour with different gluten properties, more suited to the making of cakes, pastries etc where a smaller rise and closer, finer texture are required.

For most bread the best results are obtained by using a strong plain flour. If this is not available, soft plain flour can be used instead but it will give a smaller rise and closer textured bread with a pale, hard crust and a generally disappointing result.

It is the flour used that gives each bread its characteristic flavour and texture. Nowadays there are many different flours readily available, from health food stores if not from your local supermarket or grocer.

Generally bread made with brown flour has a closer texture and a stronger, more distinctive taste than white bread. As brown flour does not store as well as white, it should be bought in smaller quantities.

Wholemeal flour contains 100 per cent wheat. The entire grain is milled, and bread made with this flour is coarse textured and has a nutty taste.

Wheatmeal flour contains 80–90 per cent wheat (ie some of the bran is removed) and it is more absorbent than white flour, giving a denser textured bread than white but not as coarse as wholemeal.

Stoneground refers to the specific process of grinding the flour which heats it and gives it a slightly roasted, nutty flavour. Both wholemeal and wheatmeal can be stoneground.

Granary flour contains malt and crushed wheat, giving a crunchy, rough texture.

Rye flour used on its own produces rather dense, heavy bread as rye lacks sufficient protein for the formation of gluten. Finely milled rye flour gives the densest texture and bread made with coarsely milled rye flour is rougher and more open-textured. The traditional German pumpernickel is made from coarsely ground rye flour. The best results for baking at home are obtained by combining the rye flour with a strong wheat flour.

Salt
Salt improves the flavour. It should be measured accurately, as too little causes the dough to rise too quickly and too much kills the yeast and gives the bread an uneven texture. Salt is used in the proportions of 5–10 ml (1–2 level tsp) to 450 g (1 lb) flour.

Fat
The addition of fat to the dough enriches it and gives a moist, close-textured loaf with a soft crust. It also helps keep the bread fresh and soft for a longer time.

Liquid
Water is most suitable for plain bread, producing a loaf with an even texture and a crisp crust. Milk and water, or milk alone, will give a softer golden crust and the loaf will stay soft and fresh for longer.

The amount of liquid used will vary according to the absorbency of the flour, as too much will give the bread a spongy and open texture. Brown flours are usually more absorbent than white.

The liquid is generally added to the yeast at a tepid temperature, ie 43°C (110°F).

Glazes and finishes
If a crusty finish is desired for bread or rolls, they can be brushed before baking with a glaze made by dissolving 10 ml (2 level tsp) salt in 30 ml (2 tbsp) water.

For a soft finish the surface should be brushed with oil and dusted with flour, or alternatively brushed with beaten egg or beaten egg and milk.

Some breads and yeast buns are glazed after baking to give them a sticky finish. To achieve this brush with warmed honey or a syrup made by dissolving 30 ml (2 level tbsp) sugar in 30 ml (2 tbsp) water; bring to the boil.

There are many ways of adding interest and variety to bread and rolls. After glazing and before baking, lightly sprinkle the surface with one of the following:

1 Poppy, caraway, celery or fennel seeds.
2 Sesame seeds. Particularly good sprinkled on to the soft baps used with hamburgers.
3 Cracked wheat or crushed cornflakes. Sprinkle them on top of wholemeal bread or baps.
4 A mixture of crushed rock salt and caraway. This is particularly good on rolls to be eaten with cheese or smoked sausage.

Step by step processes in breadmaking

The processes used in making yeast mixtures form the basis of the method followed for nearly all yeast cooking.

1 Mixing the dough
Measure all the ingredients carefully and sift the dry ingredients (flour, salt, etc) into a large bowl.

Add the yeast dissolved in the liquid all at once and mix the dry ingredients, using a wooden spoon or fork, until blended. Extra flour can be added at this stage if it is too slack. Beat the dough by hand until the mixture is completely smooth and leaves the sides of the bowl cleanly.

2 Kneading the dough
Kneading is essential to strengthen the gluten in the flour, thus making the dough elastic in texture and enabling it to rise more easily. This is how to do it:

Turn the dough on to a floured working surface, knead the dough by folding it towards you and pushing down and away from you with the palm of the hand. Give the dough a quarter turn and continue

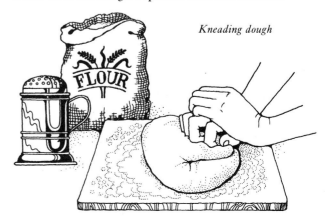

Kneading dough

kneading for about 10 minutes until it is firm, elastic and no longer sticky.

Using a dough hook If you have a mixer with a dough hook attachment it can take the hard work out of kneading. Follow manufacturer's instructions; working with small amounts of dough is more successful than attempting a large batch all at once. Place the yeast dissolved in the liquid in the bowl, add the dry ingredients and begin at lowest speed and mix to form dough. Increase the speed for the recommended time.

3 Rising

The kneaded dough is now ready for rising. Unless otherwise stated, place in a greased bowl and cover with a large sheet of polythene brushed with oil, to prevent a skin forming during rising.

Rising times vary with temperature. As only extreme heat kills the yeast and extreme cold retards the growth of yeast the method of rising can be arranged to suit yourself.

The best results are obtained by allowing the covered dough to rise overnight or up to twenty-four hours in the refrigerator. The refrigerated dough must be allowed to return to room temperature before it is shaped.

Allow about 2 hours for the dough to rise at room temperature, 18°C (65°F). The dough can be made to rise in about 45 minutes – 1 hour if placed in a warm place such as an airing cupboard or above a warm cooker. The risen dough should spring back when gently pressed with a (floured) finger.

4 Preparing tins

While the dough is rising, prepare the tins or baking sheets by greasing and lightly flouring them. Whenever reference is made to a 450 g (1 lb) loaf tin, the approximate size to use is 20.5 × 10 × 6.5 cm (8 × 4 × 2½ in), top measurements. When reference is made to a 900 g (2 lb) loaf tin, use one with 23 × 13 × 7 cm (9 × 5 × 3 in), top measurements.

5 Knocking back

The best texture is obtained by kneading the dough for a second time after rising. Turn the risen dough on to a lightly floured working surface and knead for 2–3 minutes to 'knock' out any large bubbles and ensure an even texture. The dough is shaped as required (*see page 15*) and placed in tins or on baking sheets at this stage, then covered with polythene.

6 Proving or second rise

This is the last process before baking. The shaped dough should be allowed to 'prove', that is, left until it is doubled in size and will spring back when lightly pressed with a (floured) finger. This is done at room temperature. The dough is now ready for glazing (*see page 13*) and baking.

Rising dough covered with oiled polythene

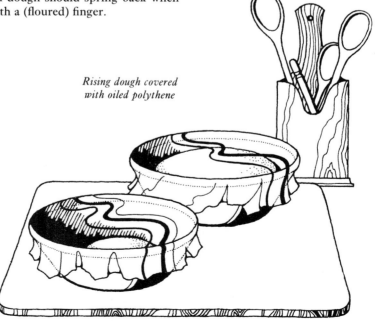

7 Baking

Basic breads are baked in the oven at 230°C (450°F), mark 8.

When cooked the bread should be well risen and golden brown and when tapped underneath with the knuckles, it should sound hollow. Allow the bread to cool on wire racks before storing.

8 Storing

Bread should be stored in an airtight tin or for longer storage *see page 17*. Dough must be stored frozen (*see page 17*).

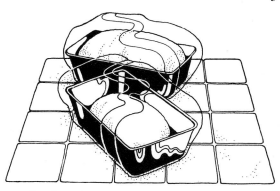

Bread proving in tins, covered with oiled polythene

9 Refreshing bread

Wrap the bread in aluminium foil and place in the oven at 230°C (450°F) mark 8, for 5–10 minutes. Allow the bread to cool in the foil before unwrapping. For a more crusty loaf omit the foil and bake as above.

To make traditional bread and roll shapes

Bread shapes

Tin loaf Roll out dough to an oblong and roll up like a Swiss roll. Tuck the ends under and place in the prepared tin. Before baking score the top of the loaf with a knife if wished.

Baton Shape into a long roll, with tapering ends, about 20.5 cm (8 in) long.

Cob Knead dough into a ball by drawing the sides down and tucking underneath to make a smooth top.

Crown Divide the dough. Knead into small pieces and place in a greased round sandwich tin. It is usually pulled apart into rolls when served.

Cottage Divide the dough into two, making one piece twice as large as the other. Knead well and shape into rounds, place smaller round on top of the larger one, and place on baking sheet. Make a hole through the middle of both pieces using the handle of a wooden spoon. Cover and leave to rise. Glaze with salt water before baking.

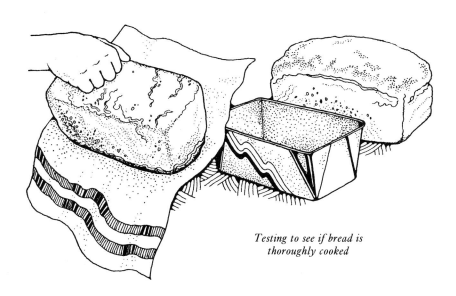

Testing to see if bread is thoroughly cooked

From top to bottom: Tin loaf   Cob   Bloomer   Crown   Bap   Baton   Cottage

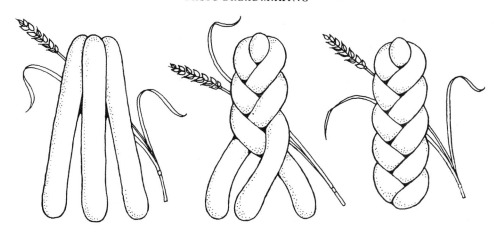

How to plait bread or rolls

Bloomer Flatten the dough and roll up like a Swiss roll. Tuck the ends under and place on baking sheet. When proved to double in size make diagonal slits on top with a sharp knife. Brush with beaten egg or salt glaze (salted water) before baking.

Plait Divide the dough into three and shape into three long rolls about 30.5 cm (12 in) long. Pinch the ends together and plait loosely crossing each strand alternately. Pinch the ends together. Place on a baking sheet and allow to prove. Before baking brush with beaten egg and sprinkle with poppy seeds.

Roll shapes
Rolls can be made in any of the traditional bread shapes by dividing the basic white dough into 50 g (2 oz) pieces and shaping as for bread. Other variations are:

Knots Shape each piece into a thin roll and tie into a knot.

Rounds Place the pieces on a very lightly floured board and roll each into a ball. To do this, hold the hand flat almost at table level and move it round in a circular motion, gradually lifting the palm to get a good round shape.

Rings Make a thin roll with each piece of dough and bend it round to form a ring; damp the ends and mould them together.

Home freezing bread and dough

Freezing baked bread
Baked loaves and rolls, both commercial and home baked, can be home frozen, and it is a successful way of storing bread for up to about one month. There are three points to remember.
1 Only freeze freshly baked bread.
2 Freezer bags are the best containers. Make sure all the air is excluded before sealing the bag tightly.
3 Label to indicate the date of freezing.

Storage times The length of storage depends on the crust, but generally bread stores well for four weeks. Bread with any form of crisp crust only stores well for about a week, then the crust begins to 'shell off'. Enriched breads and soft rolls store well for up to six weeks.

Thawing bread Leave to thaw in the sealed freezer bag (to prevent drying out) at room temperature, or overnight in the refrigerator.

To make the crust crisp Remove the freezer bag and place the thawed loaf or rolls in a fairly hot oven 230°C (450°F) mark 8, for 5–10 minutes, until the crust is crisp.

Freezing bread dough
All bread dough can be home frozen, but the storage time varies with the type of dough – plain or enriched.

Remember these four points.
1 The best results are obtained if the quantity of yeast used in the recipe is increased, for example, increase 15 g ($\frac{1}{2}$ oz) yeast to 20 g ($\frac{3}{4}$ oz).

2 Freeze the unrisen dough in the quantities you are most likely to use.
3 The most successful containers for dough are freezer bags. Oil them lightly and seal tightly. (The sealing is most important – see note below on 'skinning'.)
4 Label to indicate the date of freezing and type of dough frozen.

'Skinning' To prevent the dough forming a skin it should be tightly sealed in the freezer bag to exclude air, but, if there is a chance of the dough rising slightly before it is frozen, leave 2.5 cm (1 in) of space above the dough. A very marked skin will crack when the dough is handled, and the baked crust will have a streaked appearance. The degree of skinning also depends on the storage time : the longer the dough is kept, the more marked the skin.

Storage times Unrisen dough. Plain white dough will keep up to eight weeks; enriched white dough up to five weeks. Dough kept longer than these times gives poor results. Loss of resilience and difficulty in 'knocking back' the dough begins after about three weeks' storage; the dough is also slower to prove.

Thawing dough Thaw dough at room temperature : 18–22°C (65°–72°F). Dough can be thawed overnight in the refrigerator, but if left overnight at room temperature it will be over-risen. Thaw the dough in the freezer bag to prevent a skin forming, but first unseal the bag and then reseal it loosely at the top, to allow space for the dough to rise.

Everyday Bread

Even a beginner can make the most delicious, perfectly risen loaves without too much difficulty. There's no mystery involved: just read very carefully through the basic skills and processes described in the previous chapter and you're ready to start. Pay particular attention to the kneading and rising of the dough as these are the most crucial stages. There's a world of difference in the volume and texture of bread which has been well kneaded and allowed to rise properly, compared with bread which has not.

In this chapter you will find lots of recipes for your daily bread – the chief difference between them is in the flour used – there are so many varieties in the shops today. You will want to experiment a little once you have mastered our 'basic white bread' recipe on page 20. This is made with the hard wheat (strong bread) flour most commonly used in this country for bread but you will also find recipes using wholemeal, wheatmeal and stoneground flours and two using ryemeal flour – the dark rye recipe is particularly popular in Scandinavia and Germany. From the basic white bread you can make all the traditional shapes such as cottage, baton, twists and plaits, using different glazes and finishes (see pages 13 and 15).

The Grant bread recipe was created by Doris Grant, a founder of the natural health food cult. She believed in using the whole of the wheat for breadmaking, including the bran and the germ (otherwise known as wholemeal) and in cutting out one of the basic breadmaking processes (the second rise). This makes for a slightly less open textured bread – though you can hardly notice the difference. The end result is a filling nutty-flavoured bread which goes well with savoury foods.

White bread

This is a basic household bread recipe which lends itself to all sorts of variations.

700 g (1½ lb) strong plain flour
10 ml (2 level tsp) salt
knob of lard
15 g (½ oz) fresh yeast
400 ml (¾ pint) tepid water

Grease a 900-g (2-lb) loaf tin. Sift the flour and salt into a large bowl and rub in the lard. Blend the yeast with the water. Make a well in the centre of the dry ingredients and add the yeast liquid all at once. Stir in with a wooden fork or spoon. Work it to a firm dough, adding extra flour if needed, until it will leave the sides of the bowl clean. Do not let the dough become too stiff as this produces heavy 'close' bread.

Turn the dough on to a floured surface and knead thoroughly until the dough feels firm and elastic and no longer sticky – about 10 minutes. Shape it into a ball and place in a large bowl.

Cover the dough with lightly oiled polythene to prevent a skin forming and allow to rise (*see page 14*) until it is doubled in size and will spring back when pressed with a floured finger. Turn the risen dough on to a lightly floured surface, flatten it firmly with the knuckles to knock out the air bubbles, then knead again well. Stretch the dough into an oblong the same width as the tin, fold it into three and turn it over so that the 'seam' is underneath. Smooth over the top, tuck in the ends and place in the greased 900-g (2-lb) loaf tin.

Cover the tin with lightly oiled polythene and leave to rise until the dough comes to the top of the tin and springs back when pressed with a floured finger.

Remove the polythene, glaze and finish as desired (*see page 13*). Place the tin on a baking sheet and place in the oven.

Bake at 230°C (450°F) mark 8, for 30–40 minutes until well risen and golden brown. When the loaf is cooked it will shrink slightly from the sides of the tin, and will sound hollow if you tap the bottom of it. Turn out and cool on a wire rack.

To make rolls After knocking back the dough, divide it into about eighteen 50 g (2 oz) pieces and roll into any of the shapes described on page 17. Place on greased baking sheets about 2.5 cm (1 in) apart.

> *Note* To avoid repetition of instructions all the recipes have been written using fresh yeast. Dried yeast may be used instead – see page 12.

Cover the baking sheets with lightly oiled polythene and leave to rise until doubled in size. Remove the polythene, glaze and finish as desired (*see page 13*).

Bake at 230°C (450°F) mark 8, for 15–20 minutes, until well risen and golden brown. Cool on a wire rack.
MAKES ABOUT 18

Quick white bread

This recipe reduces the preparation time by omitting one of the 'rises'.

15 g (½ oz) fresh yeast
about 300 ml (½ pint) tepid water
450 g (1 lb) strong plain flour
5 ml (1 level tsp) salt

Grease two small loaf tins. Blend the yeast with the water. Sift the flour and salt into a bowl, make a well in the centre and add the yeast liquid. Mix to an elastic dough, adding more water if necessary. Turn on to a floured surface and knead for about 10 minutes, until really smooth. Divide the dough into two portions and put into the prepared tins; cover the tins with lightly oiled polythene and allow to rise in a warm place until the dough fills the tins and springs back when lightly pressed. Bake in the oven at 230°C (450°F) mark 8, for about 25 minutes. Turn out and cool on a wire rack.

To make rolls Divide the dough into 50 g (2 oz) pieces and proceed as above, but allow only 15–20 minutes for baking.

Enriched white bread

This is another basic dough made from strong flour and enriched with fat, eggs and milk. The resulting bread and rolls have a soft crust and more cake-like texture and keep longer than bread made from the basic white dough (see this page). It is best used for bridge rolls, baps and Hamburger buns etc.

The sponge batter method of incorporating the yeast is especially good when making an enriched white dough.

450 g (1 lb) strong plain flour
15 g (½ oz) fresh yeast
225 ml (8 fl oz) tepid milk
5 ml (1 level tsp) salt
50 g (2 oz) butter or block margarine
1 egg, beaten

Grease and flour two baking sheets. Sift 150 g (5 oz) of the flour into a large bowl. Crumble the yeast, add the milk and stir until dissolved. Add to the flour and set aside to froth – about 20 minutes.

Mix the remaining flour with the salt and rub in the fat. Add the egg and the flour mixture to the batter and mix well to give a fairly soft dough that will leave the sides of the bowl clean. Turn the dough on to a lightly floured surface and knead until it is smooth and no longer sticky – about 10 minutes. Place in a bowl. Cover the dough with lightly oiled polythene and leave to rise until doubled in size. When risen, turn the dough on to a light floured surface, knead well and shape as required into plaited loaves, baps or fancy rolls. Place on the greased and floured baking sheets. Cover with lightly oiled polythene and put to prove until doubled in size. Glaze with beaten egg and finish as desired (see page 13). Bake in the oven at 190°C (375°F) mark 5, 45–50 minutes for loaves and 10–15 minutes for rolls. Turn out and cool on a wire rack.

Wholemeal bread

50 g (2 oz) fresh yeast
900 ml (1½ pints) tepid water
1.4 kg (3 lb) plain wholemeal flour
30 ml (2 level tbsp) caster sugar
20–25 ml (4–5 level tsp) salt
25 g (1 oz) lard

Grease two 900-g (2-lb) or four 450-g (1-lb) loaf tins. Blend the yeast with 300 ml (½ pint) of the water. Mix the flour, sugar and salt together; rub in the lard. Stir the yeast liquid into the dry ingredients, adding sufficient of the remaining water to make a firm dough that leaves the bowl clean. Turn it out on to a lightly floured surface and knead until it feels firm and elastic and no longer sticky. Shape it into a ball, place in a large bowl and cover with lightly oiled polythene to prevent a skin forming. Leave the dough to rise until doubled in size. Turn it out on to a floured surface and knead again until firm. Divide into two or four pieces and flatten firmly with the knuckles to knock out any air bubbles. Knead well to make it firm and ready for shaping. Shape to fit the tins. Cover with lightly oiled polythene and leave until the dough rises almost to the tops of the tins – about 1 hour at room temperature.

Brush the tops with salt glaze and bake the loaves in the oven at 230°C (450°F) mark 8, for 30–40 minutes. Turn out and cool on a wire rack.

Different shapes
1 Divide each quarter portion of dough into four smaller pieces, shape into rolls and fit side by side into the tin. Finish as above.

2 Shape each quarter portion of dough into a round cob, dust with flour and put on a floured baking sheet. Finish as before.

3 Shape all the dough into a round cob and place on a large floured baking sheet. Cut into four wedges and scatter cracked wheat or flour over the top. Allow to rise, mark again and bake for 40–45 minutes.

Wheatmeal flowerpots

COLOUR PLATE PAGE 32

Grease two clean clay flowerpots well and bake them empty in a hot oven before use. This will prevent the loaves sticking.

450 g (1 lb) wheatmeal flour or 225 g (8 oz) each brown and white plain flours
10 ml (2 level tsp) each salt and sugar
knob of lard
15 g (½ oz) fresh yeast
300 ml (½ pint) warm water
milk to glaze
cracked wheat

Grease two 10–12.5 cm (4–5 in) flowerpots. Mix the flours, salt and sugar in a bowl, rub in the lard. Blend the yeast with the water and add to the flour, mixing to a soft dough that leaves the bowl clean. Knead the dough thoroughly on a floured surface for about 10 minutes and divide between the two greased flowerpots. Cover with lightly oiled polythene and leave to rise until doubled in size. Brush the tops lightly with milk or water and sprinkle with cracked wheat. Bake at 230°C (450°F) mark 8, for 30–40 minutes. Turn out and cool on a wire rack.

Quick wholemeal bread

15 g (½ oz) fresh yeast
about 300 ml (½ pint) tepid water
5 ml (1 level tsp) sugar
450 g (1 lb) wholemeal flour or 225 g (8 oz) wholemeal and 225 g (8 oz) strong plain flour
5–10 ml (1–2 level tsp) salt
25 g (1 oz) lard

Grease two baking sheets. Blend the yeast with the water. Mix the sugar, flour and salt and rub in the lard. Add the yeast liquid and remaining water and mix with a wooden spoon to give a fairly soft dough, adding more water if necessary. Turn it on to a floured surface and knead well. Divide the dough into two, shape into rounds and place on the greased baking sheets. Cover with lightly oiled polythene and leave to rise until the two rounds have doubled in size. Bake in the oven at 230°C (450°F) mark 8, for about 15 minutes, reduce the heat to 200°C (400°F) mark 6, and cook for a further 20–30 minutes. Turn out and cool on a wire rack.

Grant bread

This is excellent for sandwiches as it is a moist bread which keeps well for several days and can be used for a further few days as toast. Fresh yeast and sugar are used in this recipe to give a quick fermentation.

450 g (1 lb) stoneground wholemeal flour
5 ml (1 level tsp) salt
5 ml (1 level tsp) sugar
15 g ($\frac{1}{2}$ oz) fresh yeast
215 ml (13 fl oz) tepid water

Grease one 900-g (2-lb) loaf tin well and place in a warm oven. Mix the salt with the flour. Combine the yeast with the sugar, add a quarter of the water, and leave for 10 minutes until frothy. Pour the yeast liquid into the flour, add the rest of the water and mix very well with a wooden spoon – or by hand, which is the best method.

Half-fill the tin with the dough, and place in a warm place, covered with lightly oiled polythene. Leave until the dough has risen nearly to the top of the tin. Bake in the oven at 200°C (400°F) mark 6, for 35–40 minutes. Turn out and cool on a wire rack.

Light rye bread

350 g (12 oz) white rye flour
5 ml (1 level tsp) sugar
15 g ($\frac{1}{2}$ oz) fresh yeast
25 mg ascorbic acid tablet,* crushed
200 ml (7 fl oz) warm water
15 ml (1 level tbsp) caraway seeds
5 ml (1 level tsp) salt
knob of margarine

For the glaze
2.5 ml ($\frac{1}{2}$ level tsp) cornflour
boiling water

---

*Ascorbic acid tablets are obtainable from chemist shops.

Grease a loaf tin with 21.5 × 11 cm ($8\frac{3}{4}$ × $4\frac{3}{8}$ in) top measurements. Mix together 100 g (4 oz) flour, the sugar, yeast, ascorbic acid tablet and water. Stand in a warm place, covered, for 1 hour. Mix the caraway seeds and salt with the remaining flour and rub in the margarine.

Combine the dry mixture with the yeast mixture, and work to a soft dough. Knead on a lightly floured working surface for 5 minutes. Cover with lightly oiled polythene and leave to rise for about 1 hour in a warm place. Knead lightly and shape into a loaf, place in the greased loaf tin. Cover and leave to rise in a warm (if possible steamy) atmosphere for about 30 minutes. Bake in the oven at 180°C (350°F) mark 4, 30 minutes, then brush with glaze made by blending the cornflour with a little cold water then adding enough boiling water to clear and thicken. Return to the oven for a further 20 minutes. Turn out and wrap in a tea towel to cool.

Dark rye bread

This is a dark hearty loaf with a light texture made with equal quantities of rye and wheat flour. It is particularly good with savoury foods such as ham, sausage or cheese.

275 g (10 oz) rye flour
275 g (10 oz) plain flour
15 g ($\frac{1}{2}$ oz) salt
10 ml (2 level tsp) caraway or fennel seeds
150 ml ($\frac{1}{4}$ pint) tepid water
150 ml ($\frac{1}{4}$ pint) tepid milk
15 ml (1 tbsp) black treacle
25 g (1 oz) fresh yeast

For the glaze
beaten egg
water

Grease two baking sheets. Sift the flour and salt together into a mixing bowl. Stir in the caraway or fennel seeds. Combine the water, milk and treacle, crumble in the yeast and stir until blended. Pour into the flour mixture and mix to form a firm dough. adding extra flour if required. Turn the dough on to a lightly floured surface and knead until the dough feels smooth and elastic. Place in a bowl, cover with lightly oiled polythene and leave to rise until the dough has doubled in size.

Turn the risen dough on to a lightly floured surface, knead well and divide into two. Shape into traditional cob or baton shape (*see page 15*). Place on greased baking sheets and cover with lightly oiled polythene.

Leave to prove until doubled in size and the dough springs back when lightly pressed with a floured finger.

Bake in the oven at 190°C (375°F) mark 5, for 30 minutes. Brush the top with the egg and water mixture and reduce the heat to 180°C (350°F) mark 4, for a further 20 minutes. The loaf should be brown and sound hollow when tapped on the base. Cool on a wire rack.

Oatmeal bread

This Old English bread is known as Clapbread in Lancashire. It is generally eaten with cheese but is also particularly good toasted and served hot and buttered. It keeps fresh and moist for several days – store in an airtight tin.

225 g (8 oz) oatmeal, medium or rolled
300 ml (½ pint) milk
15 g (½ oz) fresh yeast
75 ml (5 tbsp) tepid water
350 g (12 oz) strong plain flour
15 ml (3 level tsp) salt
30 ml (2 tbsp) oil

For the glaze
milk
oatmeal

Grease two 450-g (1-lb) loaf tins. Soak the oatmeal in the milk for 30 minutes. Crumble the yeast into a small basin, add the water and stir until dissolved. Mix together the soaked oatmeal, flour, salt and oil. Add the yeast mixture and beat to a soft but firm dough. Turn the dough on to a lightly floured surface and knead thoroughly until firm and elastic. Place in a bowl and cover with oiled polythene. Leave to rise until doubled in size.

Turn the risen dough on to a floured surface, knead lightly and divide into two portions. Flatten each piece and roll up like a Swiss roll. Place the dough in the two greased loaf tins. Cover with oiled polythene and leave to rise to the top of the tins. Brush the tops with milk and sprinkle with oatmeal. Bake in the oven at 230°C (450°F) mark 8, for 30 minutes.

Reduce the heat to 150°C (300°F) mark 2, and bake for a further 30 minutes. Remove from the tins and allow to cool on a wire rack.

Note To avoid repetition of instructions all the recipes have been written using fresh yeast. Dried yeast may be used instead – see page 12.

Poppy seed plait

COLOUR PLATE PAGE 32

450 g (1 lb) strong plain flour
15 g (½ oz) fresh yeast
225 ml (8 fl oz) tepid milk
5 ml (1 level tsp) salt
50 g (2 oz) butter or block margarine
1 egg, beaten

For the glaze and topping
beaten egg
poppy seeds

Lightly grease a baking sheet. Put 150 g (5 oz) of the flour into a large bowl. Crumble the yeast, add the milk and stir until dissolved. Add to the flour and mix well. Set aside in a warm place until frothy – about 20 minutes. Mix the remaining flour with the salt and rub in the fat. Add the egg and the flour mixture to the yeast batter and mix well to give a fairly soft dough that will leave the sides of the bowl clean. Turn the dough on to a lightly floured surface and knead until smooth and no longer sticky – about 10 minutes (no extra flour should be necessary). Place in a bowl, cover with lightly oiled polythene and leave to rise until doubled in size. Knead the dough again lightly on a floured working surface, divide in half and roll each half into an oblong. Cut each half into three strips lengthwise, pinching the dough together at the top. Plait the strips, damp the ends and seal together. Place on the lightly greased baking sheet. Brush with the egg and sprinkle with poppy seeds. Prove again until doubled in size. Bake in the oven at 190°C (375°F) mark 5, for 45–50 minutes. Cool on a wire rack.

Cheese pull-aparts

COLOUR PLATE PAGE 32

225 g (8 oz) strong plain flour
2.5 ml (½ level tsp) salt
5 ml (1 level tsp) dry mustard
50 g (2 oz) Cheddar cheese, grated
25 g (1 oz) butter or block margarine
50 g (2 oz) celery or onion, finely chopped
15 g (½ oz) fresh yeast
150 ml (¼ pint) milk

For the glaze
beaten egg

Grease a tin 18 × 24.5 × 4.5 cm (7 × 9¾ × 1¾ in). Mix together the flour, salt, mustard and cheese. Heat the fat and sauté the celery or onion gently until soft. Add to the dry ingredients. Blend the yeast with the milk, add to the dry ingredients and work to a firm dough. Knead for 10 minutes. Place in a bowl, cover with lightly oiled polythene. Leave to rise until doubled in size. Turn out and knead again. Cut into eight equal-sized pieces, shape into finger-shaped pieces.

Cut down the length of each with a sharp knife to about 0.5-cm (¼-in) depth. Place side by side in the tin, not quite touching. Cover with lightly oiled polythene and leave to rise in a warm place – about 45 minutes. Brush with beaten egg and bake at 190°C (375°F) mark 5, for about 25 minutes. Cool on a wire rack. Break apart and serve buttered.

Floury baps

15 g (½ oz) fresh yeast
300 ml (½ pint) milk and water mixed
450 g (1 lb) strong plain flour
5 ml (1 level tsp) salt
50 g (2 oz) lard

Lightly flour a baking sheet. Blend the yeast with the liquid. Sift together the flour and salt and rub in the lard. Stir in the yeast liquid. Work the mixture to a firm dough, adding extra flour only if really needed, until the dough leaves the sides of the bowl clean. Knead on a floured surface for about 5 minutes. Place in a large bowl and cover with lightly oiled polythene and allow to rise until doubled in size. Lightly knead the dough, then cut into eight to ten even-sized pieces. Shape each into a ball, place on the floured baking sheet and press down to flatten slightly. Cover with

oiled polythene and allow to rise until doubled in size – about 45 minutes at room temperature. Dredge the tops lightly with flour and bake at 200°C (400°F) mark 6, for 15–20 minutes. Cool on a wire rack.

Bridge rolls

15 g (½ oz) fresh yeast
100 ml (4 fl oz) tepid milk
225 g (8 oz) plain flour
5 ml (1 level tsp) salt
50 g (2 oz) butter or block margarine
1 egg, beaten

For the glaze (optional)
beaten egg

Grease a baking sheet. Blend the yeast with the milk. Mix the flour and salt and rub in the fat. Add the yeast liquid and egg and mix to a fairly soft dough, adding a little extra milk if necessary. Beat well and knead the dough on a floured surface until smooth. Place in a bowl and cover with lightly oiled polythene. Leave to rise until doubled in size. Knead lightly on a floured surface, then cut into twelve to sixteen pieces. Make each into a tapered roll shape and place fairly close together in rows on the baking sheet. Allow to rise for 15–20 minutes. Brush with beaten egg if a glazed finish is required and bake in the oven at 220°C (425°F) mark 7, for about 15 minutes. Allow to cool on a wire rack before breaking apart. Bridge rolls should be served absolutely fresh.

Fancy Breads and Bakes

These special breads are yeast mixtures enriched with fat or egg. Fruit or spices are often added and the dough is then moulded into fancy shapes. The 'sponge dough' process is often used for these mixtures: yeast and liquid are added to a small amount of the flour and allowed to froth before the remaining flour and ingredients are added. The idea of making bread for tea originated with the baker putting aside a portion of his first batch of ordinary bread dough to 'dress up' for tea with dried fruit, special glazes or whatever he had to hand. The Fruit ring recipe on page 33 is a good example of a traditional enriched bread.

Brioches and croissants are two of the French equivalents of our enriched breads. There are dozen of variations of brioches – the recipe we have given is one of the popular versions you are most likely to come across when travelling on the Continent. Croissants have a light flaky texture and are particularly delicious eaten hot, straight from the oven, as they do in France, with lots of unsalted butter.

Another recipe you might not have tried making is crumpets. If you have always bought them before from the local baker we recommend you have a go at making your own. The recipe is quite straightforward: it's a simple yeast batter cooked on a griddle. The only special equipment you will need are the traditional crumpet rings to pour the mixture into to prevent the batter spreading – many hardware stores stock them. Once the crumpets are cooked, the traditional way to serve them is toasted – before an open fire if you are lucky enough to have one, if not, a toaster or grill will do just as well. Once toasted, spread crumpets with butter straight away so that the butter melts and soaks right into them.

SHAPING CROISSANTS

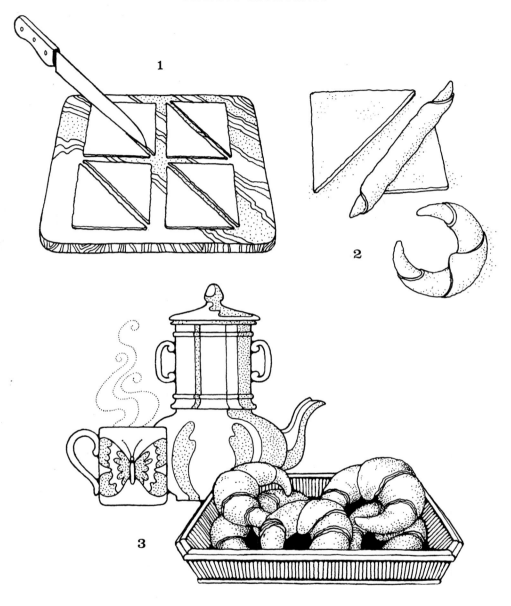

1 *Cutting dough into triangles*
2 *Rolling and curving into crescent shapes*
3 *Finished croissants*

Malt bread

25 g (1 oz) fresh yeast
about 350 ml ($\frac{3}{4}$ pint less 4 tbsp) tepid water
450 g (1 lb) plain flour (not strong plain flour)
5 ml (1 level tsp) salt
45 ml (3 tbsp) malt extract
30 ml (2 tbsp) black treacle
25 g (1 oz) butter or margarine
225 g (8 oz) sultanas

For the glaze (optional)
15 ml (1 level tbsp) sugar
15 ml (1 tbsp) water

Grease two loaf tins with 20.5 × 10 cm (8 × 4 in) top measurements. Blend the yeast into the water. Sieve the flour and salt together. Warm the malt, treacle and fat until just melted. Stir the yeast liquid and malt mixture into the dry ingredients and combine well. Stir in the sultanas and beat thoroughly for about 5 minutes. Turn the mixture into the two 20.5 × 10-cm (8 × 4-in) top measurement loaf tins. Cover and leave to rise in a warm place for about 45 minutes, or until the dough almost fills the tins. Bake in the oven at 200°C (400°F) mark 6, for 40–45 minutes. When cooked the loaves may be brushed with the sugar glaze made by dissolving the sugar in the water, and heating gently.

Croissants

Croissants are the classic crisp, flaky rolls served for a Continental breakfast, and are best eaten hot. They reheat quite well if lightly wrapped in foil. The secret of success in making them lies in layering the fat well, chilling the pastry while it is standing, to keep it firm, and working quickly so that the dough does not become too warm and soft through overhandling. The pastry is only allowed to rise at a warmer temperature after shaping.

25 g (1 oz) fresh yeast
300 ml ($\frac{1}{2}$ pint) water less 60 ml (4 tbsp)
450 g (1 lb) strong plain flour
10 ml (2 level tsp) salt
25 g (1 oz) lard
1 egg, beaten
100–175 g (4–6 oz) butter

For the glaze
1 egg
about 10 ml (2 tsp) water
2.5 ml ($\frac{1}{2}$ level tsp) caster sugar

Blend the yeast with the water. Sift together the flour and salt and rub in the lard. Add the yeast liquid and egg and mix well together. Knead on a lightly floured surface until the dough is smooth, 10–15 minutes. Roll the dough into a strip about 51 × 20.5 × 0.5 cm (20 × 8 × $\frac{1}{4}$ in) taking care to keep the edges straight and the corners square.

Soften the butter with a knife, then divide into three. Use one part to dot over the top two-thirds of the dough, leaving a small border clear. Fold in three by bringing up the plain (bottom) third first, then folding the top third over. Turn the dough so that the fold is on the right-hand side. Seal the edges with a rolling pin.

Re-shape to a long strip by gently pressing the dough at intervals with a rolling pin. Repeat with the other two portions of butter. Cover the dough with oiled polythene to prevent it forming a skin or cracking. Allow to 'rest' in the refrigerator for 30 minutes. Roll out as before, and repeat the folding and rolling three more times. Place in the refrigerator for at least 1 hour.

Roll the dough out to an oblong about 55 × 33 cm (22 × 13 in). Cover with lightly oiled polythene and leave for 10 minutes. Trim with a sharp knife to 53 × 30.5 cm (21 × 12 in) and divide in half lengthwise. Cut each strip into six triangles 15 cm (6 in) high and with a 15-cm (6-in) base. To make the glaze beat the egg, water and sugar together. Brush glaze over the triangles then roll each one loosely from the base, finishing with the tip underneath. Curve into a crescent shape.

Put the shaped croissants on to ungreased baking sheets. Brush the tops with egg glaze, cover each baking sheet inside lightly oiled polythene and leave it at room temperature for about 30 minutes, until light and puffy. Brush again with egg glaze before baking in the oven at 220°C (425°F) mark 7, for about 20 minutes.

Brioches

15 g ($\frac{1}{2}$ oz) fresh yeast
25 ml (1$\frac{1}{2}$ tbsp) warm water
225 g (8 oz) strong plain flour
pinch of salt
15 ml (1 level tbsp) caster sugar
2 eggs, beaten
50 g (2 oz) butter, melted

For the glaze
beaten egg

Oil twelve 7.5-cm (3-in) fluted patty tins. Blend the

SHAPING BRIOCHES

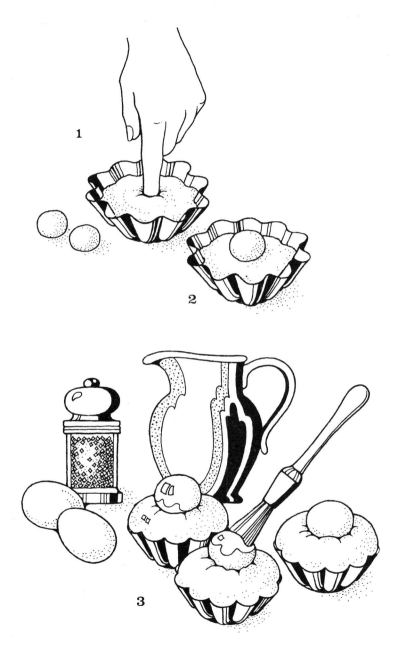

1   *Pressing a hole in the centre of the brioche*
2   *Brioche topped with small ball of dough, ready for rising*
3   *Lightly brushing brioche with egg glaze before baking*

yeast with the water. Mix together the flour, salt and sugar. Stir the yeast liquid into the flour, with the eggs and butter. Work to a soft dough, turn out on to a floured surface and knead for about 5 minutes. Place the dough in a bowl and cover with oiled polythene. Leave to rise until it is doubled in size and springs back when gently pushed with a floured finger. Knead the risen dough well on a lightly floured surface. Divide the dough into twelve pieces. Shape three-quarters of each piece into a ball and place in the patty tins. Press a hole in the centre of each. Shape the remaining dough into knobs and place in the holes. Press down lightly.

Cover the tins with oiled polythene and leave at room temperature until the dough is light and puffy and nearly reaches the top of the tins. Brush lightly with the egg glaze and bake in the oven at 230°C (450°F) mark 8, for about 10 minutes, until golden. Turn out and cool on a wire rack.

Swedish tea ring

COLOUR PLATE PAGE 49

½ **quantity of risen enriched white bread dough**
   (*see page 20*)
15 g (½ oz) butter, melted
50 g (2 oz) brown sugar
10 ml (2 level tsp) powdered cinnamon
glacé cherries, angelica and/or flaked
   almonds

For the glacé icing
100 g (4 oz) icing sugar, sifted
water
lemon juice

Grease a baking sheet. Roll the dough to an oblong 30.5 × 23 cm (12 × 9 in). Brush with melted butter, then sprinkle the mixed brown sugar and cinnamon

SWEDISH TEA RING

1   *Rolling up along the long edge*
2   *Cutting slashes with scissors at intervals*
      round the ring

over the dough. Roll up tightly from the long edge and bend round to form a ring and seal the ends together. Place on the baking sheet; using scissors, cut slashes at an angle 2.5 cm (1 in) apart and to within 1 cm (½ in) of the inside edge. Twist the cut sections to overlap each other. Cover with lightly oiled polythene and put to rise in a warm place for about 30 minutes. Bake in the oven at 190°C (375°F) mark 5, for 30–35 minutes. Ice and decorate (see below) and cool on a wire rack.

To make the glacé icing, blend the icing sugar with a good squeeze of lemon juice and just enough water to give a thick coating consistency. While the ring is still warm dribble icing over it with a spoon. Decorate with cherries, angelica 'leaves' and/or nuts.

Christmas fruit loaf

15 g (½ oz) fresh yeast
150 ml (¼ pint) tepid water
450 g (1 lb) strong plain flour
5 ml (1 level tsp) salt
10 ml (2 level tsp) mixed spice
25 g (1 oz) caster sugar
350 g (12 oz) mixed dried fruit
25 g (1 oz) blanched almonds, finely chopped
grated rind and juice of 1 large orange
2 eggs beaten

For the glaze
orange marmalade

Grease a 900-g (2-lb) loaf tin or two 450-g (1-lb) tins. Crumble the yeast, add the water and stir until blended. Sift together the flour, salt, spice and sugar, then mix in the dried fruit and nuts. Add the orange juice and rind, the yeast mixture and the eggs, then mix the dough. Knead well on a floured surface until firm and elastic. Put the dough into a bowl and cover with oiled polythene, leave to rise until nearly doubled in size and springy to the touch. Turn the risen dough on to a floured surface, knead for 2–3 minutes, then shape to fit the prepared tin(s). Leave to rise again until almost doubled in size. Bake in the oven at 200°C (400°F) mark 6, for 20 minutes, then reduce to 190°C (375°F) mark 5, and continue to bake

Note To avoid repetition of instructions all the recipes have been written using fresh yeast. Dried yeast may be used instead – see page 12.

for about 30 minutes for a large loaf, 10–15 minutes for the smaller loaves. Turn out on to a wire rack and brush the bread while still warm with melted orange marmalade.

Rum babas

25 g (1 oz) fresh yeast
90 ml (6 tbsp) tepid milk
225 g (8 oz) strong plain flour
2.5 ml (½ level tsp) salt
30 ml (2 level tbsp) caster sugar
4 eggs, beaten
100 g (4 oz) butter, soft but not melted
100 g (4 oz) currants
whipped cream

For the rum syrup
120 ml (8 tbsp) clear honey
120 ml (8 tbsp) water
rum or rum essence to taste

Lightly grease about sixteen 9-cm (3½-in) ring tins with lard. Crumble the yeast into a basin. Add the tepid milk and stir well until dissolved. Pour over 50 g (2 oz) of the flour in a bowl and blend until smooth. Allow to stand in a warm place until frothy – about 20 minutes. Add the remaining flour, the salt, sugar, eggs, butter and currants, and beat well for 3–4 minutes. Half-fill the tins with the dough, cover with oiled polythene and allow to rise until the moulds are two-thirds full. Bake in the oven at 200°C (400°F) mark 6, for 15–20 minutes. Cool for a few minutes, then turn out on to a wire rack. While the babas are still hot, spoon over each enough rum syrup (see below) to soak it well. Leave to cool. Serve with whipped cream in the centre.

To make the rum syrup warm together the honey and water and add rum (or rum essence) to taste.

Savarin
Make up the Rum baba mixture as described above, omitting the currants, put into greased 20.5-cm (8-in) ring tin.

Bake in the oven at 200°C (400°F) mark 6, for about 40 minutes, or until golden and shrinking away from the sides of the tin. Turn out straight away and allow to cool. Make rum syrup as for the Rum baba recipe. Soak the Savarin with syrup. Brush with sieved apricot jam and serve on a dish surrounded by fruit salad and topped with whipped cream.

1   *Half-filled tins covered with oiled polythene*   2   *Rum syrup being spooned over each baba*
3   *Cream being piped into baba rings*   4   *Finished baba*

CRUMPETS

1   *Pouring the batter into the crumpet rings*
2   *Finished crumpets ready for toasting*

Crumpets

COLOUR PLATE OPPOSITE

350 g (12 oz) strong plain flour
15 g ($\frac{1}{2}$ oz) fresh yeast
300 ml ($\frac{1}{2}$ pint) warm water
about 200 ml (7 fl oz) milk
2.5 ml ($\frac{1}{2}$ level tsp) bicarbonate of soda
5 ml (1 level tsp) salt
oil or lard for greasing

Place half the flour in a bowl with the yeast and warm water. Blend until smooth, cover and leave until frothy – about 20 minutes. Stir in the remaining ingredients gradually, beating until smooth. Add more milk if necessary to make a pouring batter. Grease a griddle or heavy shallow frying pan, and about six crumpet rings or metal cutters, 7.5-cm (3-in) in diameter. Heat thoroughly. Pour about 30 ml (2 tbsp) of the batter into the rings on the hot griddle.

Wheatmeal flowerpots · Poppy seed plait
Cheese pull-aparts · Crumpets ▶

Cook until set and holes are formed then remove rings and turn crumpets over to brown the other side lightly. Cool on a wire rack. Toast lightly on both sides and serve hot and buttered.

MAKES ABOUT 16

For preparation of griddle see page 51.

Hungarian coffee cake

For the dough
450 g (1 lb) strong plain flour
5 ml (1 level tsp) sugar
15 g ($\frac{1}{2}$ oz) fresh yeast
225 ml (8 fl oz) warm milk
5 ml (1 level tsp) salt
50 g (2 oz) butter or block margarine
1 egg, beaten

For the topping
40 g ($1\frac{1}{2}$ oz) butter, melted
75 g (3 oz) caster sugar
5 ml (1 level tsp) ground cinnamon
25 g (1 oz) shelled walnuts, chopped
25 g (1 oz) seedless raisins

Grease a 1.7-litre (3-pint) ring mould. In a large bowl blend together 150 g (5 oz) flour, sugar, yeast and milk to give a batter. Leave in a warm place until frothy – about 20 minutes. Sift the remaining flour into the salt and rub in the fat. Add the egg and the flour mixture to the batter and mix well to give a fairly soft dough that leaves the sides of the bowl clean. Turn the dough on to a lightly floured surface and knead until it is smooth and no longer sticky – about 10 minutes. Place the dough in a lightly greased polythene bag, loosely tied, and allow to rise until doubled in size. Turn the dough on to a lightly floured surface and knead lightly. Divide the dough into twenty-four equal pieces and roll into balls the size of a walnut.

Roll each ball in the melted butter. Toss each ball in a mixture of sugar, cinnamon, walnuts and raisins. Arrange a double row of balls in the greased ring mould. Cover with oiled polythene and leave to rise to the top of the ring mould – about 45 minutes in a warm place. Bake at 200°C (400°F) mark 6, for about 25 minutes. Cool for a few minutes, turn out carefully on to a wire rack.

Note To avoid repetition of instructions all the recipes have been written using fresh yeast. Dried yeast may be used instead – see page 12.

Coburg buns · Madeira cake · Banbury cakes
Coventry God cakes · Devonshire splits

Glazed cinnamon whirl

1 recipe quantity Hungarian coffee cake dough
(see left).

For the filling
grated rind of 1 orange
30 ml (2 tbsp) orange juice
7.5 ml ($1\frac{1}{2}$ level tsp) ground cinnamon
50 g (2 oz) icing sugar
water
glacé icing to decorate, optional

Grease a 1.7-litre (3-pint) loaf tin. Cover dough with oiled polythene and leave to rise until doubled in size. Work the grated rind and juice into the risen dough. Roll out to a rectangle 15 × 33 cm (6 × 13 in) on a lightly floured surface. Brush surface lightly with water and sprinkle with cinnamon and sugar. Roll up tightly from the short edge and place in the greased loaf tin. Cover with oiled polythene and leave to rise for about 25 minutes until dough reaches the top of the tin. Bake at 200°C (400°F) mark 6, for about 30 minutes until well risen. Turn out and cool on a wire rack. When cold, drizzle the curved surface of the roll with glacé icing, if wished.

Fruit ring

$\frac{1}{2}$ recipe quantity Hungarian coffee cake dough
(see left)

For the filling
25 g (1 oz) butter, melted
50 g (2 oz) soft brown sugar
50 g (2 oz) sultanas
50 g (2 oz) currants
50 g (2 oz) chopped mixed peel
2.5 ml ($\frac{1}{2}$ level tsp) ground cinnamon
beaten egg

For the decoration
50 g (2 oz) icing sugar
little egg white

Grease a baking sheet. Cover dough with oiled polythene and leave to rise until doubled in size. Turn on to a floured surface, knead lightly. Roll out the dough to a rectangle 25.5 × 51 cm (10 × 20 in). Brush with melted butter, sprinkle with sugar blended with sultanas, currants, peel and cinnamon. Roll up from the long side. Place on greased baking sheet, joined edge down. Brush the ends with beaten egg and join together firmly. Using scissors, snip the dough at intervals and pull each point of dough down the side of the ring. Brush with more beaten egg. Cover loosely with oiled polythene and leave to rise until doubled in size. Bake at 190°C (375°F) mark 5, for about 30 minutes. Just before the end of the cooking time, make up a little stiff but flowing icing with the icing sugar and egg white. Brush over surface of ring, return to the oven for a few minutes. Cool on a wire rack.

Apricot and walnut loaf

½ recipe quantity of risen wheatmeal flowerpot
   dough (*see page 21*)
25 g (1 oz) caster sugar
100 g (4 oz) dried apricots, chopped
50 g (2 oz) walnut halves, broken

For the crumble topping
25 g (1 oz) butter
25 g (1 oz) caster sugar
40 g (1½ oz) plain flour

Base line and grease a 450-g (1-lb) loaf tin. In a bowl, squeeze and work together with one hand all the ingredients (except those for the topping), until thoroughly mixed. Two-thirds fill the prepared tin and cover with oiled polythene until the dough rises almost to the top of the tin. Cover with a topping made by lightly rubbing together the butter, sugar and flour until the mixture resembles coarse breadcrumbs. Bake in the oven at 200°C (400°F) mark 6, for 40–45 minutes. Cool in the tin for 10 minutes, then turn out on to a wire rack.

Traditional Recipes

Our country is rich in traditional cakes and bakes. Not just every county and town but practically every village has its own recipe or its own particular way of making a well-known cake or bun or pastry. We have chosen recipes for some old favourites, such as Eccles cakes and Bath buns, for which everyone needs the perfect recipe, and others, less well known but no less delicious, which you may not have heard of unless you are lucky enough to live in the right place. How many people outside (or even inside) Coventry have heard of Coventry God cakes, for example? Do you know they are rich pastry enclosing mincemeat, rather like Eccles cakes, and that the cuts traditionally slashed on top were to let the devil (and the steam) out. Everyone's heard of Sally Lunn, but do you know she was probably a figment of the imagination and that the word, according to Dorothy Hartley in *Food in England** was a corruption of the cry 'Soleil et Lune' (literally, sun and moon – the seller's vivid description of the wares she was selling). The Black bun is one of Scotland's most satisfying cakes – packed with dried fruit and enclosed in thin pastry just strong enough to hold the fruit in. There are many versions of it and we've included one that we know is good. Many traditional British recipes are made from a yeast mixture – you'll find it helpful to turn to page 12 and re-read the basics of yeast cookery before trying the recipes in this chapter.

*Macdonald and Jane's (£3.95 in paperback)

Chelsea buns

Saffron cake

The Phoenicians introduced saffron to Cornwall where this cake is believed to originate.

25 g (1 oz) fresh yeast
150 ml (¼ pint) tepid milk
450 g (1 lb) strong plain flour
5 ml (1 level tsp) salt
50 g (2 oz) butter
50 g (2 oz) lard
175 g (6 oz) currants
grated rind of ½ lemon
25 g (1 oz) caster sugar
small pkt (10 grains) of ground saffron, infused overnight in 150 ml (¼ pint) boiling water

Grease a 20.5-cm (8-in) round cake tin. Crumble the yeast into a small basin, stir in the milk. Mix the flour and salt and rub in the butter and lard. Stir in the currants, lemon rind and sugar. Strain the saffron infusion into a pan and warm slightly; pour into the other ingredients, add the milk and yeast mixture and beat well. Turn the dough into the tin, cover with oiled polythene and leave in a warm place to rise until nearly at the top of the tin – about 1 hour. Bake in the oven at 200°C (400°F) mark 6, for 30 minutes, reduce to 180°C (350°F) mark 4, and bake for a further 30 minutes. Turn out and cool on a wire rack.

Chelsea buns

These were an 18th-century speciality of the Old Chelsea Bun House in Pimlico which was then in the borough of Chelsea.

225 g (8 oz) strong plain flour
15 g (½ oz) fresh yeast
100 ml (4 fl oz) tepid milk
2.5 ml (½ level tsp) salt
about 15 g (½ oz) butter or lard
1 egg, beaten
melted butter
75 g (3 oz) dried fruit
30 ml (2 level tbsp) chopped mixed peel
50 g (2 oz) soft brown sugar
clear honey to glaze

Grease an 18-cm (7-in) square cake tin. Put 50 g (2 oz) of the flour in a large bowl. Blend together the yeast and milk until smooth. Add to the flour, mix well and set aside in a warm place until frothy – 15–20 minutes. Mix the remaining flour and salt; rub in the fat. Mix into the batter with the egg to give a fairly soft dough that will leave the sides of the bowl clean after beating. Turn the dough out on to a lightly floured surface and knead until smooth – about 5 minutes. Put in a greased bowl. Cover with oiled polythene and leave to rise for 1–1½ hours.

Knead the dough and roll out to an oblong

30 × 23 cm (11¾ × 9 in). Brush with melted butter and cover with a mixture of dried fruit, peel and brown sugar. Roll up from the longest side like a Swiss roll, and seal the edge with water. Cut into nine equal-sized slices and place these, cut side down, in the prepared cake tin. Prove until the dough has doubled in size and feels springy to the touch. Bake the buns in the oven at 190°C (375°F) mark 5, for about 30 minutes. While they are still warm, brush them with a wetted brush dipped in honey.

London buns

These little, orange flavoured yeast buns also became popular in the 18th century at the fashionable Old Chelsea Bun House in Pimlico.

450 g (1 lb) strong plain flour
pinch of nutmeg
50 g (2 oz) caster sugar
40 g (1½ oz) butter
300 ml (½ pint) tepid milk
15 g (½ oz) fresh yeast
30 ml (2 level tbsp) chopped mixed peel
grated rind of 1 orange

For the glaze
beaten egg
coarse sugar

Grease a baking sheet. Sift the flour and nutmeg into a large basin and stir in the sugar. Melt the butter in a saucepan and add the milk. Crumble yeast into a basin, pour on the milk mixture and stir until dissolved. Pour into the centre of the flour, add the peel and orange rind and mix to make a fairly soft dough. Turn on to a floured surface and knead well, until the dough feels firm and elastic. Place in the basin and cover with oiled polythene. Leave to rise until doubled in size. Turn on to a floured surface and knead well, divide into twelve pieces and knead each piece into round buns. Put them on a greased baking sheet and leave to prove until doubled in size. Bake in the oven at 200°C (400°F) mark 6, for about 30 minutes.

Five minutes before the end of cooking time, brush the tops with beaten egg and sugar and return to oven

Note to avoid repetition of instructions all the recipes have been written using fresh yeast. Dried yeast may be used instead – see page 12.

to glaze. Cool on a wire rack.
MAKES 12 BUNS

Hot cross buns

These are traditionally eaten on Good Friday. The symbolic crosses are usually made of pastry, but, if you prefer, mark them on with a sharp knife.

450 g (1 lb) strong plain flour
25 g (1 oz) fresh yeast
150 ml (¼ pint) tepid milk
60 ml (4 tbsp) tepid water
5 ml (1 level tsp) salt
2.5 ml (½ level tsp) mixed spice
2.5 ml (½ level tsp) powdered cinnamon
2.5 ml (½ level tsp) grated nutmeg
50 g (2 oz) caster sugar
50 g (2 oz) butter, melted and cooled, but not firm
1 egg, beaten
100 g (4 oz) currants
30–45 ml (2–3 level tbsp) chopped mixed peel
50 g (2 oz) shortcrust pastry (*see page 89*)

For the glaze
60 ml (4 tbsp) milk and water
45 ml (3 level tbsp) caster sugar

Flour a baking sheet. Put 100 g (4 oz) of the flour in a large mixing bowl. Crumble the yeast into a mixing bowl. Pour over the liquid, stir until dissolved. Add to the flour and mix well. Set aside in a warm place until frothy – about 15–20 minutes. Sift together the remaining 350 g (12 oz) flour, salt, spices and sugar. Stir the butter and egg into the frothy yeast mixture, add the spiced flour and the fruit, and mix together. The dough should be fairly soft. Turn it out on to a

Hot cross buns

slightly floured surface and knead until smooth. Place in a bowl and cover with oiled polythene. Leave to rise until doubled in size.

Turn the risen dough out on to a floured working surface and knead to knock out the air bubbles. Divide the dough into twelve pieces and shape into buns, using the palm of one hand. Press down hard at first on the table surface, then ease up as you turn and shape the buns. Arrange them well apart on the floured baking sheet, and prove until doubled in size. Roll out the pastry thinly on a floured surface and cut into thin strips about 9 cm (3½ in) long. Damp the pastry strips and lay two on each bun to make a cross. Bake in the oven at 190°C (375°F) mark 5, for 15–20 minutes, until golden brown and firm to the touch. Meanwhile, heat the milk and water and sugar gently together. Brush the hot buns twice with glaze, then leave to cool.

MAKES 12

Lardy cake

This filling enriched dough recipe from Wiltshire (also known as 'Shaley cake') can be served straight from the oven as a pudding or as a cake for tea. Left over Lardy cake can be toasted or refreshed by reheating in a closed biscuit tin in a hot oven for about 10 minutes.

15 g (½ oz) fresh yeast
300 ml (½ pint) tepid water
450 g (1 lb) strong plain flour
10 ml (2 level tsp) salt
cooking oil
50 g (2 oz) butter
100 g (4 oz) caster sugar
5 ml (1 level tsp) powdered mixed spice
75 g (3 oz) sultanas or currants
50 g (2 oz) lard

Grease a tin which measures 25.5 × 20.5 × 5 cm (10 × 8 × 2 in). Blend the yeast with the water. Sift the flour and salt into a basin and stir in the yeast mixture with 15 ml (1 tbsp) oil to give a manageable soft dough. Beat until smooth. Cover with oiled polythene and leave to rise until doubled in size.

Turn the dough out on to a lightly floured surface and knead for 5–10 minutes. Roll out to a strip 0.5 cm (¼ in) thick. Cover two-thirds of the dough with small flakes of butter and 45 ml (3 tbsp) sugar, and sprinkle with half the spice and half the dried fruit. Fold and roll out as for flaky pastry (*see page 89*). Repeat the process with the lard, 45 ml (3 tbsp) sugar and the remaining spice and fruit. Fold and roll once more.

Place the dough in the prepared tin, pressing it down so that it fills the corners. Cover, and leave to rise in a warm place until doubled in size. Brush with oil, sprinkle with the remaining caster sugar and mark criss-cross fashion with a knife. Bake in the oven at 220°C (425°F) mark 7, for about 30 minutes. Cool on a wire rack. Serve sliced, plain or with butter.

Bath buns

These were created in Bath in the 18th century at the time when it was fashionable for the rich to 'take the waters' at Bath Spa.

450 g (1 lb) strong plain flour
25 g (1 oz) fresh yeast
150 ml (¼ pint) tepid milk
60 ml (4 tbsp) tepid water
5 ml (1 level tsp) salt
50 g (2 oz) caster sugar
50 g (2 oz) butter, melted and cooled, but not firm
2 eggs, beaten
175 g (6 oz) sultanas
30–45 ml (2–3 level tbsp) chopped mixed peel

For the topping
beaten egg
crushed sugar lumps

Grease two baking sheets. Put 100 g (4 oz) of the flour in a large mixing bowl. Crumble the yeast into a small basin, pour over the liquid and stir until dissolved. Add to the 100 g (4 oz) flour and mix well. Set aside in a warm place until frothy – about 20 minutes. Sift together the remaining flour and salt and add the sugar. Stir the butter and eggs into the yeast mixture, add the remaining flour mixture, sultanas and peel and mix well. The dough should be fairly soft. Turn it out on to a floured surface and knead until smooth. Place in a bowl and cover with oiled polythene and leave to rise until doubled in size. Beat well by hand. Place in about eighteen spoonfuls on the greased baking sheets, cover with oiled polythene and leave to rise. Brush with egg and sprinkle with crushed sugar. Bake in the oven at 190°C (375°F) mark 5, for about 15 minutes, until golden. Cool on a wire rack and serve buttered.

MAKES ABOUT 18

> *Note* To avoid repetition of instructions all the recipes have been written using fresh yeast. Dried yeast may be used instead – see page 12.

Sally Lunn

COLOUR PLATE PAGE 49

50 g (2 oz) butter
200 ml (7 fl oz) tepid milk
5 ml (1 level tsp) caster sugar
2 eggs
15 g (½ oz) fresh yeast
450 g (1 lb) strong plain flour
5 ml (1 level tsp) salt

For the glaze
60 ml (4 tbsp) water
30 ml (2 level tbsp) sugar

Thoroughly grease two 12.5-cm (5-in) round cake tins. Melt the butter slowly in a pan, remove from the heat and add the milk and sugar. Beat the eggs and add with the warm milk mixture to the yeast. Blend well. Add to the flour and salt, mix well and lightly knead. Put into the cake tins, cover with oiled polythene and leave to rise until the dough fills the tins – about 45 minutes–1 hour. Bake in the oven at 230°C (450°F) mark 8, for 15–20 minutes. Turn the Sally Lunns out of the tins on to a wire rack. Make the glaze by heating the water and sugar to boiling point and boiling for 2 minutes. Use at once to glaze the hot buns.

Doughnuts

15 g (½ oz) fresh yeast
about 60 ml (4 tbsp) tepid milk
225 g (8 oz) plain flour
2.5 ml (½ level tsp) salt
knob of butter or margarine
1 egg, beaten
thick jam
deep fat for frying
sugar and ground cinnamon to coat

Blend the yeast with the milk. Mix the flour and salt and rub in the fat. Add the yeast liquid and egg and mix to a soft dough, adding a little more milk if necessary. Beat well until smooth, cover with oiled polythene and leave to rise until doubled in size. Knead lightly on a floured surface and divide into ten to twelve pieces. Shape each into a round, put 5 ml (1 tsp) thick jam in the centre and draw up the edges to form a ball, pressing firmly to seal them together. Heat the fat to 180°C (360°F) or until it will brown a 2.5-cm (1-in) cube of bread in 1 minute. Fry the doughnuts fairly quickly until golden brown (for 5–10 minutes, according to size). Drain on

crumpled kitchen paper and toss in sugar mixed with a little cinnamon (if you like). Serve the same day they are made.
MAKES 10–12

Devonshire splits

COLOUR PLATE PAGE 33

15 g (½ oz) fresh yeast
about 300 ml (½ pint) tepid milk
450 g (1 lb) strong plain flour
5 ml (1 level tsp) salt
50 g (2 oz) butter
30 ml (2 level tbsp) sugar

To serve
jam and Devonshire or whipped cream
icing sugar

Grease a baking sheet. Blend the yeast with half the milk. Mix the flour and salt, warm the butter and sugar in the remaining milk and when at blood heat, stir into a well in the centre of the flour with the yeast liquid. Beat to an elastic dough, turn it out on to a floured surface and knead until smooth. Place in a bowl and cover with oiled polythene. Allow to rise until doubled in size, then turn it on to a lightly floured surface and divide into fourteen to sixteen pieces. Knead each lightly into a ball, place on a greased baking sheet and flatten slightly with the hand. Put to rise in a warm place for about 20 minutes and bake in the oven at 220°C (425°F) mark 7, for 15–20 minutes. Turn out on to a wire rack. Before serving split them and spread one half with jam and Devonshire or whipped cream, sandwich together again and sprinkle the tops with icing sugar.
MAKES 14–16

Yorkshire tea cakes

15 g (½ oz) fresh yeast
300 ml (½ pint) tepid milk
450 g (1 lb) strong plain flour
5 ml (1 level tsp) salt
50 g (2 oz) butter or block margarine
25 g (1 oz) caster sugar
100 g (4 oz) currants
25 g (1 oz) chopped mixed peel
milk for glazing

Grease two baking sheets. Crumble the yeast and pour on the milk. Stir until dissolved. Mix the flour and salt, rub in the fat and stir in the sugar, currants and peel. Add the yeast liquid to give a fairly soft

dough. Beat well and knead on a lightly floured surface for about 10 minutes, until smooth. Place in a bowl and cover with oiled polythene. Allow to rise until doubled in size. Turn on to a lightly floured surface and divide into five equal pieces. Knead lightly into rounds and roll each out to a round 15–18 cm (6–7 in) across. Put on the baking sheets and brush the tops with milk. Cover with oiled polythene and allow to rise for 45 minutes, until almost doubled in size. Bake in the oven at 200°C (400°F) mark 6, for about 20 minutes. Cool on a wire rack. To serve, split in two and butter well, or split, toast and serve hot and buttered.
MAKES 5

Coventry God cakes

COLOUR PLATE PAGE 33

Small, triangular-shaped mincemeat tarts. Traditionally made and given by Godparents to their Godchildren on New Year's Eve.

½ **quantity of puff pastry** (*see page 90*)
120 ml (8 level tbsp) mincemeat

For the glaze
egg white, beaten
caster sugar

Roll out the pastry to about 0.5 cm (¼ in) thick. Cut the pastry into triangles and place a spoonful of mincemeat in the centre of half of them. Damp the edges of these and top with a triangular lid. Press the edges well together. Make a slit in the top and glaze with egg white, then dredge with caster sugar. Place on a baking sheet. Bake in the oven at 200°C (400°F) mark 6, for about 20 minutes. Cool on a wire rack.

Eccles cakes

½ **quantity puff pastry** (*see page 90*)

For the filling
25 g (1 oz) butter, softened
25 g (1 oz) soft brown sugar
25 g (1 oz) finely chopped mixed peel
50 g (2 oz) currants

For the glaze
egg white
caster sugar

Roll out the pastry thinly and cut into 9-cm (3½-in) rounds. Bind the ingredients for the filling and place a small spoonful of mixture in centre of each pastry round. Draw up the edges together and reshape into a round. Turn it over and roll lightly until the currants just show through. Score with a knife in a lattice pattern. Allow the cakes to 'rest' on a baking sheet for about 10 minutes in a cool place. Brush them with egg white and dredge with caster sugar. Bake in the oven at 230°C (450°F) mark 8, for about 15 minutes, until golden. Cool on a wire rack.
MAKES ABOUT 8

Coburg buns

COLOUR PLATE PAGE 33

6 blanched almonds
150 g (5 oz) plain flour
5 ml (1 level tsp) bicarbonate of soda
2.5 ml (½ level tsp) gound allspice
2.5 ml (½ level tsp) ground ginger
2.5 ml (½ level tsp) ground cinnamon
50 g (2 oz) butter or block margarine
50 g (2 oz) caster sugar
1 egg, beaten
15 ml (1 tbsp) golden syrup
60 ml (4 tbsp) milk

Grease twelve fluted bun tins and place half an almond in each. Sift together the flour, bicarbonate of soda and spices. Cream together the fat and sugar until light and fluffy. Add the egg a little at a time, beating well after each addition. Mix the syrup and milk and add alternately with the flour, folding in lightly until evenly mixed. Divide the mixture between the tins and bake in the oven at 180°C (350°F) mark 4, for about 25 minutes, until firm to the touch. Turn out and cool on a wire rack. Eat while fresh.
MAKES 12

Banbury cakes

COLOUR PLATE PAGE 33

½ **quantity puff pastry** (*see page 90*)
50 g (2 oz) currants
50 g (2 oz) raisins, stoned
15 ml (1 level tbsp) flour
25 g (1 oz) chopped mixed peel
50 g (2 oz) demerara sugar
2.5 ml (½ level tsp) powdered nutmeg
2.5 ml (½ level tsp) powdered cinnamon
25 g (1 oz) butter, melted

For the glaze
beaten egg white
15–30 ml (1–2 level tbsp) caster sugar

BANBURY CAKES

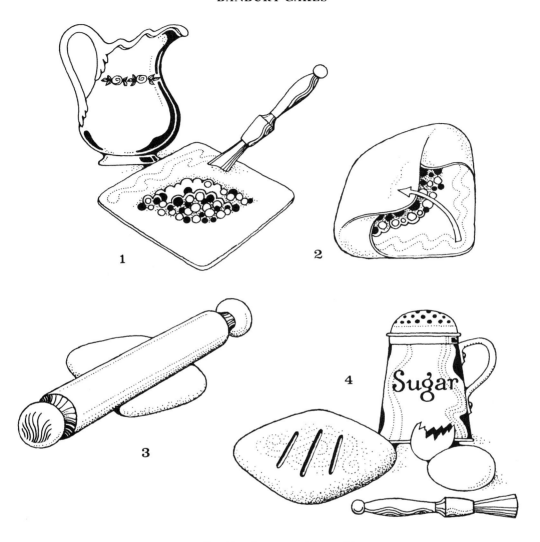

1   *Brushing the pastry with egg white*
2   *Drawing pastry edges to the centre*
3   *Rolling lightly to shape*
4   *Finished cake*

Mix the fruit, flour, peel, sugar and spices with the butter. Roll out the pastry thinly and cut into six to eight 12.5-cm (5-in) rounds. Place 15 ml (1 level tbsp) of fruit mixture in the centre of each pastry round. Brush the edges of the pastry with the egg white and draw them up to the centre. Press well to enclose the filling. Turn the cakes over and roll lightly until the fruit just shows under the pastry and the cakes are oval in shape (*see diagrams 1–3 above*).

Make several cuts in the top of each cake, forming a criss-cross pattern. Brush the tops with egg white and sprinkle with caster sugar.

Place on a baking sheet and bake in the oven at 220°C (425°F) mark 7, for about 20 minutes, or until the pastry is golden brown. Cool on a wire rack.
MAKES 6–8 CAKES

SHORTBREAD

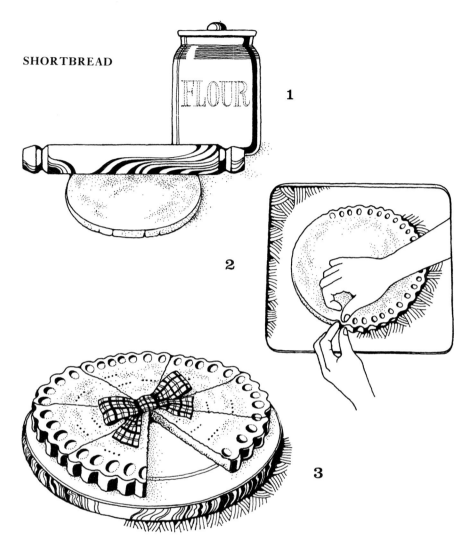

1   *Rolling shortbread to size*
2   *Crimping the edges of the shortbread*
3   *Finished shortbread*

Shortbread

175 g (6 oz) plain flour, or 100 g (4 oz) plain
  flour and 50 g (2 oz) rice flour
pinch of salt
100 g (4 oz) butter
50 g (2 oz) caster sugar

Grease and base line one 15–18 cm (6–7 in) sandwich
tin with greaseproof paper. Sift together the flour and
salt. Rub in the butter and add the sugar. Continue
lightly kneading the mixture until it forms a dough.
Roll or press out to fit the tin, crimp the edges of the
shortbread and mark across into six to eight portions
and prick neatly with a fork. Bake in the oven at
170°C–180°C (325°–350°F) mark 3–4, for about 40
minutes–1 hour, until just coloured. Cool on a wire
rack. Dredge with caster sugar and break into
portions when cold.

Alternatively, shape the mixture into a round and bake on a papered baking sheet, or use a shortbread mould for shaping. To use a shortbread mould, flour the mould liberally, press shortbread into it, turn the shortbread out on to a baking sheet (the mould does not go into the oven) by knocking sides of mould on folded cloth. In this case, cool on the baking sheet.

Parkin

225 g (8 oz) plain flour
10 ml (2 level tsp) baking powder
10 ml (2 level tsp) ground ginger
50 g (2 oz) butter or block margarine
50 g (2 oz) lard
225 g (8 oz) medium oatmeal
100 g (4 oz) caster sugar
175 g (6 oz) golden syrup
175 g (6 oz) treacle
60 ml (4 tbsp) milk

Grease and line a tin measuring 25.5 × 20.5 × 4 cm (10 × 8 × $1\frac{1}{2}$ in).

Sift together the flour, baking powder and ginger. Rub in the fat. Add the oatmeal and sugar. Heat together the syrup and treacle until warm, make a well in the dry ingredients and stir in the syrup, treacle and milk. Mix until smooth, then pour into the tin. Bake in the oven at 180°C (350°F) mark 4, for 45 minutes – 1 hour. The mixture will shrink away from the sides of the tin and may dip slightly in the centre. Turn out and cool on a wire rack.

Keep for at least a week before eating and, if liked, serve sliced and buttered.

Simnel cake

450 g (1 lb) (ready-made weight) almond
  paste (*see page 107*)
225 g (8 oz) plain flour
pinch of salt
2.5 ml ($\frac{1}{2}$ level tsp) grated nutmeg
2.5 ml ($\frac{1}{2}$ level tsp) powdered cinnamon
225 g (8 oz) currants
100 g (4 oz) sultanas
75 g (3 oz) chopped mixed peel
100 g (4 oz) glacé cherries, quartered
175 g (6 oz) butter
175 g (6 oz) caster sugar
3 eggs
milk to mix, if required
egg white or sieved apricot jam

Grease and line an 18-cm (7-in) round cake tin. Shape one-third of the almond paste into a round slightly smaller than the cake tin.

Sift together the flour, salt and spices. Mix the currants, sultanas, peel and cherries. Cream the butter and sugar until pale and fluffy and beat in each egg separately. Fold the flour into the creamed mixture, adding a little milk, if required, to give a dropping consistency. Fold in the fruit. Put half the mixture into the prepared tin and place the round of almond paste on top. Cover with the rest of the mixture, spreading it evenly. Bake in the oven at 150°C (300°F) mark 2, for $2\frac{1}{2}$–3 hours, until the cake is a rich brown and firm to the touch. Leave to cool on a wire rack.

From the remaining almond paste, shape eleven small balls, then make the rest into a round to fit the top of the cake. Brush the top surface of the cake with egg white or sieved jam, place the almond paste round in position and smooth it slightly with a rolling pin. Pinch the edges into scallops with finger and thumb. Score the surface with a knife, arrange the almond paste balls in position round the edge and if liked for extra glaze brush the whole with egg white. Grill until light golden brown and finish with a ribbon and a bow when cold.

Maids of honour

These small cakes were first made in Henry VIII's palace at Hampton Court where they proved so popular with the Queen's maids of honour that they were named after them.

568 ml (1 pint) milk
15 ml (1 tbsp) rennet
$\frac{1}{2}$ quantity puff pastry (*see page 90*)
1 egg, beaten
15 g ($\frac{1}{2}$ oz) butter, melted
50 g (2 oz) caster sugar

Prepare a junket in the usual way with the milk and rennet. When set, put in a muslin bag and leave to drain overnight. Remove the curd from the bag well before it is required – it should be really firm. Roll out the pastry very thinly – and cut out twelve rounds using a 7.5-cm (3-in) plain cutter. Line twelve 6.5-cm ($2\frac{1}{2}$-in) patty tins with the pastry, pressing at the base so that it is paper thin; prick the bottom of the pastry well. Stir the egg, butter and sugar into the drained curd. Divide the mixture between the patty tins, then bake in the oven at 200°C (400°F) mark 6, for 30 minutes, or until well-

risen and just firm to the touch. Cool on a wire rack.
MAKES 12

Madeira cake

COLOUR PLATE PAGE 33

100 g (4 oz) plain flour
150 g (5 oz) self-raising flour
175 g (6 oz) butter or block margarine
175 g (6 oz) caster sugar
5 ml (1 tsp) vanilla essence
3 large eggs, beaten
15–30 ml (1–2 tbsp) milk
2–3 thin slices citron peel

Grease and line an 18-cm (7-in) cake tin. Sift the flours together. Cream the fat, sugar and essence until pale and fluffy. Beat in the egg a little at a time. Fold in the sifted flour, adding a little milk if necessary to give a dropping consistency. Put into the tin and place the citron peel on top. Bake in the oven at 170°C (325°F) mark 3, for about 1 hour 10 minutes. Cool for a short time in the tin, turn out and continue to cool on a wire rack.

Variations

Orange cake Omit the vanilla essence. Add the grated rind of 2 oranges to the butter and sugar.

Lemon cake Omit the vanilla essence. Add the grated rind and juice of ½ lemon with the flour.

Rich seed cake Omit the vanilla essence and citron peel. Add 10 ml (2 level tsp) caraway seeds with the flour. Dredge with granulated sugar before baking.

Dream cake Omit the citron peel. Add 75 g (3 oz) chopped walnuts and 75 g (3 oz) quartered glacé cherries with the flour.

Dundee cake

225 g (8 oz) plain flour
pinch of salt
225 g (8 oz) butter
225 g (8 oz) caster sugar
4 large eggs, beaten
350 g (12 oz) sultanas
350 g (12 oz) currants
175 g (6 oz) chopped mixed peel
100 g (4 oz) small glacé cherries
grated rind of ½ lemon
50–75 g (2–3 oz) whole blanched almonds

Grease and line a 20.5-cm (8-in) round cake tin. Sift together the flour and salt. Cream the butter, add the sugar and beat together until light and fluffy. Gradually add the beaten eggs one at a time. Fold in the flour, cleaned fruit, peel, cherries, lemon rind and 25 g (1 oz) of the nuts, chopped. Turn the mixture into the prepared tin and level the surface. Split the remainder of the nuts in half and arrange neatly over the cake, rounded side uppermost. Bake in the oven at 150°C (300°F) mark 2, for about 2½ hours. Cool on a wire rack.

Battenburg cake

175 g (6 oz) butter or block margarine
175 g (6 oz) caster sugar
vanilla essence
3 eggs, beaten
175 g (6 oz) self-raising flour
15 g (½ oz) cocoa
milk to mix, if necessary
raspberry jam or jelly
350 g (12 oz) ready-made almond paste (*see page 107*)
caster sugar

Grease and line a Swiss roll tin measuring 30.5 × 20.5 × 2 cm (12 × 8 × ¾ in) and divide it lengthwise with a 'wall' of greaseproof paper or kitchen foil. Cream the fat and sugar together until light and fluffy and add a little essence. Gradually add the eggs a little at a time, beating well after each addition. When all the egg has been added, lightly fold in the flour, using a metal spoon. Turn half of the mixture into one side of the tin. Fold the sifted cocoa into the other half, with a little milk if necessary, and spoon this mixture into the second side of the tin. Bake in the oven at 190°C (375°F) mark 5, for 40–45 minutes, until well-risen. Turn out and cool on a wire rack.

When the two parts of the cake are cold, trim them to an equal size and cut each in half lengthwise. Spread the sides of the strips with jam and stick them together, alternating the colours. Press the pieces well together, then coat the whole of the outside of the cake with jam. Roll out the almond paste thinly on caster sugar or between sheets of non-stick paper, forming it into an oblong about 35.5 × 25.5 cm (14 × 10 in). Wrap the paste completely round the cake, press firmly against the side and trim the edges. Pinch with the thumb and forefinger along the outer edges and score the top of the cake with a sharp knife to give a criss-cross pattern.

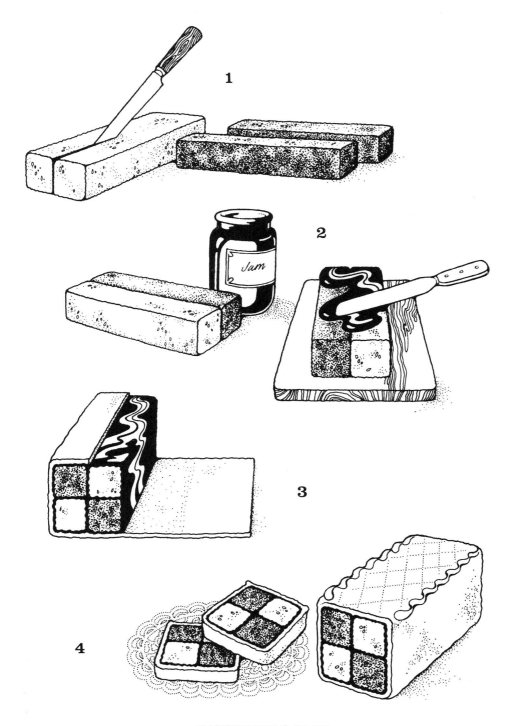

BATTENBURG CAKE

1   *Cutting each cake into two lengthwise*
2   *Spreading with jam to stick cakes together*
3   *Wrapping almond paste completely round the sides of the cake*
4   *Finished cake*

Singin' hinny

COLOUR PLATE PAGE 48

*This Northumbrian favourite hisses when turned –
hence the name.*

350 g (12 oz) plain flour
50 g (2 oz) ground rice
50 g (2 oz) sugar
5 ml (1 level tsp) salt
10 ml (2 level tsp) baking powder
25 g (1 oz) lard
75 g (3 oz) currants
150 ml ($\frac{1}{4}$ pint) milk
150 ml ($\frac{1}{4}$ pint) single cream

Preheat a griddle (*see page 51*) on preparation of
griddle). Mix together the flour, ground rice, sugar,
salt and baking powder. Rub in the lard. Mix in the
currants, then stir in the milk and cream. Roll out
the dough into a 20.5 cm (8 in) round. Prick with a
fork and cook slowly (about 20 minutes on each side)
on the griddle until golden brown. To turn Singin'
hinny over, place a baking sheet on top, reverse on to
the baking sheet then slide 'hinny' back on to the
griddle. Carefully split and serve buttered, cut in
wedges, while still warm.

Black bun

This traditional Hogmanay cake should be made several weeks or even months before it is to be eaten, so that it may mature and mellow.

For the pastry
250 g (9 oz) self-raising flour
good pinch of salt
75 g (3 oz) butter
cold water to mix

For the filling
450 g (1 lb) raisins
450 g (1 lb) currants
50 g (2 oz) chopped mixed peel
50 g (2 oz) whole almonds, blanched and halved
100 g (4 oz) caster sugar
225 g (8 oz) self-raising flour
5 ml (1 level tsp) ground ginger
5 ml (1 level tsp) ground cinnamon
1.25 ml ($\frac{1}{4}$ level tsp) black pepper
75 ml (5 tbsp) whisky
75 ml (5 tbsp) milk

For the glaze
beaten egg

Sift the flour and salt into a basin. Rub in the butter until the mixture resembles fine breadcrumbs. Stir in enough water to mix to a soft dough. Roll out two-thirds of the pastry and use to line a 19-cm (7$\frac{1}{2}$-in) round loose-bottomed cake tin. Combine all the ingredients for the filling and press into the pastry case. Press the top of the pastry over the filling, brush with water to moisten. Roll out remaining pastry and use to top the filling. Press well at the edges to seal and brush top with beaten egg. Bake in the oven at 180°C (350°F) mark 4, for about 2 hours. Allow to cool in the tin before removing.

Bakewell tart

$\frac{1}{2}$ quantity puff pastry (*see page 90*)
75 g (3 oz) sponge cake*
grated rind and juice of $\frac{1}{2}$ lemon
75 g (3 oz) ground almonds
50 g (2 oz) butter
50 g (2 oz) caster sugar
1 egg, beaten
15–30 ml (1–2 level tbsp) raspberry jam

Roll the pastry out thinly to line a 23-cm (9-in) pie plate, then leave it to 'rest' in a cool place while preparing the filling. Crumble and sift the sponge cakes; add the lemon rind and ground almonds. Cream the butter and caster sugar until light and fluffy and add the beaten egg a little at a time. Fold in the cake crumb mixture a spoonful at a time. Add enough lemon juice to give a soft dropping consistency. Spread the jam over the pastry base. Spread the crumb mixture evenly over the jam. Bake in the oven at 220°C (425°F) mark 7, for about 15 minutes, then reduce the oven temperature to 180°C (350°F) mark 4, and bake for a further 30 minutes.

*Small trifle sponge cakes are suitable.

Scones and Teabreads

Although most of us think of household bread as leavened with yeast, many people, particularly in country areas of Scotland and Ireland, still prefer the taste of soda bread. This bread is so called because it is made with bicarbonate of soda (plus cream of tartar and butter milk) instead of yeast. It was traditionally cooked on a griddle over an open peat fire.

The griddle – or girdle as it is sometimes called – is a special large flat pan with a heavy base and heavy curved handle. It distributes heat evenly and holds it well, which makes it particularly good for cooking over the open fire. Today soda breads are more often cooked on a baking sheet in the oven, and if you haven't got a griddle use any heavy flat based pan. If you are lucky enough to have a griddle, though, don't forget to prepare it properly before using it for the first time (see our instructions on page 51). This preparation, or 'seasoning' as it is properly called is most important because it seals up the hundreds of tiny pores in the metal and so stops the bread or scones from sticking. Old-fashioned iron griddles should be kept lightly oiled to prevent them rusting.

We have included teabreads in this chapter because, like soda bread and scones, they are part of the traditional 'high tea'. This meal of meat, bread and cake is particularly popular in the north though many of the teabread recipes actually originated in North America. Teabreads are often made by the 'rubbing-in' method – that is, by rubbing the fat into the flour before adding the other ingredients such as dates, raisins, nuts and spices. Serve them like scones – fresh, split or sliced and thickly buttered. Eat them with jam or honey or, for a change, try them the traditional northern way – with cheese.

Singin' hinny · Date scone bars
Treacle scones · Wholemeal scone round ▶

Oven scones

A preheated baking sheet aids the rise of scones. Place the baking sheet in the oven when you start preparing the mixture. Lightly grease the sheet before placing the scones on it (this is not necessary if you are using a non-stick surface).

**225 g (8 oz) self-raising flour
5 ml (1 level tsp) baking powder
1.25 ml ($\frac{1}{4}$ level tsp) salt
40 g (1$\frac{1}{2}$ oz) butter or block margarine
40 g (1$\frac{1}{2}$ oz) sugar
50 g (2 oz) currants
about 150 ml ($\frac{1}{4}$ pint) milk**

Preheat a baking sheet. Sift the flour, baking powder and salt into a mixing bowl. Cut the fat into small pieces and add to the flour. Rub in the fat with the fingertips until no lumps are left and the mixture looks like fine breadcrumbs. Stir in the sugar and the cleaned fruit, then add most of the milk 15 ml (1 tbsp) at a time, stirring well with a round-bladed knife until the mixture begins to stick together. Using one hand, collect the mixture together and knead it lightly to form a smooth, fairly soft dough. Turn it out on to a lightly floured surface, form into a flat, round shape and roll out 2 cm ($\frac{3}{4}$ in) thick. Cut into 5-cm (2-in) rounds, put on the baking sheet and brush the tops with a little milk. Bake in the hottest part of the oven at 230°C (450°F) mark 8, for about 10 minutes, until well risen and golden. Cool on a wire rack; serve split and buttered.

MAKES 10–12

Sultana scones

If you wish to use self-raising flour, replace the bicarbonate of soda and cream of tartar by 5 ml (1 level tsp) baking powder, and use fresh, not soured, milk.

**225 g (8 oz) plain flour
2.5 ml ($\frac{1}{2}$ level tsp) bicarbonate of soda
2.5 ml ($\frac{1}{2}$ level tsp) cream of tartar
pinch of salt
40 g (1$\frac{1}{2}$ oz) butter or block margarine
25 g (1 oz) sugar
50 g (2 oz) sultanas
about 150 ml ($\frac{1}{4}$ pint) soured milk**

Preheat a baking sheet. Sift together the flour, bicarbonate of soda, cream of tartar and salt. Rub in the fat until the mixture resembles fine bread-crumbs. Add the sugar and sultanas. Mix with the soured milk to form a light, manageable dough. Turn on to a lightly floured surface and knead lightly. Roll out to about 2 cm ($\frac{3}{4}$ in) thick and stamp out into 6.5-cm (2$\frac{1}{2}$-in) rounds. Re-roll the scraps lightly and stamp out more rounds. Brush the scones with milk and place on the baking sheet. Bake in the oven at 230°C (450°F) mark 8, for 10–15 minutes. Cool on a wire rack.

MAKES ABOUT 9

Floury scones

**225 g (8 oz) self-raising flour
2.5 ml ($\frac{1}{2}$ level tsp) salt
50 g (2 oz) butter
1 egg, beaten
75 ml (5 tbsp) milk**

Preheat a baking sheet. Mix the flour and salt together in a bowl. Rub in the butter until the mixture resembles fine breadcrumbs. Make a well in the centre and drop in the egg; mix with a round-bladed knife. Add the milk and mix with a knife to a smooth soft dough. Turn it on to a floured surface and knead lightly to remove any cracks. Lightly press out into a round 1 cm ($\frac{1}{2}$ in) thick, then cut into eight triangles. Re-form into a round on the baking sheet and dredge with flour. Bake in the oven at 220°C (425°F) mark 7, for 10–15 minutes. Wrap in a clean tea towel and cool on a wire rack.

MAKES 8

Wholemeal scone round

COLOUR PLATE PAGE 48

**15 ml (3 level tsp) baking powder
pinch of salt
50 g (2 oz) plain flour
50 g (2 oz) caster sugar
175 g (6 oz) plain wholemeal flour
50 g (2 oz) butter or block margarine
about 150 ml ($\frac{1}{4}$ pint) milk**

Preheat a baking sheet. Sift together the baking powder, salt and plain flour into a bowl. Add the sugar and the wholemeal flour. Lightly rub in the fat, then mix to a soft but manageable dough with the milk. Knead lightly on a floured surface. Shape into a flat 15-cm (6-in) round and mark with the back

Marmalade mace teabread · Sally Lunn · Swedish tea ring

of a floured knife into six triangles. Place on the baking sheet and bake at once in the oven at 230°C (450°F) mark 8, for about 15 minutes. Serve warm, split and buttered.

Note If you wish to use self-raising wholemeal flour, reduce the amount of baking powder in the recipe to 5 ml (1 level tsp).

Date scone bars

COLOUR PLATE PAGE 48

225 g (8 oz) plain flour
2.5 ml (½ level tsp) bicarbonate of soda
5 ml (1 level tsp) cream of tartar
pinch of salt
50 g (2 oz) butter or block margarine
25 g (1 oz) sugar
75 g (3 oz) dates, stoned
about 150 ml (¼ pint) milk

Preheat a baking sheet. Sift together the dry ingredients. Rub in the fat until the mixture resembles fine breadcrumbs; add the sugar. Using kitchen scissors, snip the dates into small pieces and add to the mixture. Mix to a light dough with the milk. Roll out into an oblong 30.5 × 10 cm (12 × 14 in). Brush with milk and place on the baking sheet. Mark into eight bars, using the back of a knife. Bake in the oven at 230°C (450°F) mark 8, for about 15 minutes. Break apart and cool on a wire rack.
MAKES 8

Treacle scones

COLOUR PLATE PAGE 48

225 g (8 oz) self-raising flour
5 ml (1 level tsp) baking powder
5 ml (1 level tsp) mixed spice +5ml Cinnamon
pinch of salt
25–50 g (1–2 oz) butter or block margarine
25 g (1 oz) sugar (1 Tbl Demerara)
15 ml (1 level tbsp) black treacle
about 150 ml (¼ pint) milk 100ml Full Fat Milk
1 Tbl Sultanas
Preheat a baking sheet. Sift together the flour, baking powder, spice and salt. Rub in the fat until the mixture resembles fine breadcrumbs. Add the sugar. Warm the treacle and mix with the milk, then use to make a light, manageable dough. Roll out to about 2 cm (¾ in) thick and stamp out into 6.5-cm (2½-in) rounds. Brush with milk, place on the baking sheet and bake in the oven at 230°C (450°F) mark 8, for 10–15 minutes. 220
MAKES ABOUT 10

Soda bread

450 g (1 lb) plain flour
10 ml (2 level tsp) bicarbonate of soda
10 ml (2 level tsp) cream of tartar
5 ml (1 level tsp) salt
25–50 g (1–2 oz) lard
about 300 ml (½ pint) soured milk or
   buttermilk

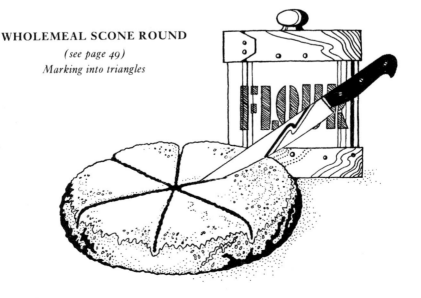

WHOLEMEAL SCONE ROUND
(see page 49)
Marking into triangles

Grease and flour a baking sheet. Sift together the dry ingredients twice. Rub in the lard. Mix to a soft but manageable dough with the milk: the amount required will depend on the absorbency of the flour. Shape into an 18-cm (7-in) round and mark into triangles. Place on the baking sheet and bake in the oven at 220°C (425°F) mark 7, for about 30 minutes. Eat while fresh.

Irish soda bread

350 g (12 oz) wholemeal plain flour
100 g (4 oz) plain flour
5–10 ml (1–2 level tsp) salt
5 ml (1 level tsp) caster sugar
5 ml (1 level tsp) bicarbonate of soda
15 g ($\frac{1}{2}$ oz) butter or block margarine
10 ml (2 level tsp) cream of tartar
300 ml ($\frac{1}{2}$ pint) milk

For the glaze
beaten egg or top of the milk to glaze

Grease and flour a baking sheet. Sift the flours, salt, sugar and bicarbonate of soda into a mixing bowl. Rub in the fat. Dissolve the cream of tartar in the milk and bind the ingredients well together, adding more milk if necessary.

Turn on to a floured surface and knead lightly to a firm, smooth dough. Flatten out to a circle 18 cm (7 in) in diameter. Place on the floured baking sheet. Glaze the surface with beaten egg or milk and mark a cross on the top. Bake in the oven at 200°C (400°F) mark 6, for about 40 minutes. Cool on a wire rack. Serve very fresh, sliced and buttered.

Wheatmeal muffins

250 g (9 oz) wheatmeal plain flour
175 g (6 oz) plain flour
5 ml (1 level tsp) baking powder
2.5 ml ($\frac{1}{2}$ level tsp) salt
100 g (4 oz) sugar
5 ml (1 level tsp) bicarbonate of soda
300 ml ($\frac{1}{2}$ pint) milk
25 g (1 oz) butter
30 ml (2 tbsp) golden syrup

Grease eighteen deep patty tins 5-cm (2-in) in diameter. Place the wheatmeal flour into a mixing bowl. Sift together the plain flour, baking powder and salt. Add to the wheatmeal flour with the sugar. Dissolve the bicarbonate of soda in the milk. Gently

heat the butter and the syrup; combine with the milk. Pour the liquid into the dry ingredients and stir well. Fill the patty tins two-thirds full. Bake in the oven at 220°C (425°F) mark 7, for 15–20 minutes.
MAKES 18

Griddle scones

If you do not possess a 'griddle' or 'girdle', use a thick-bottomed frying pan or the solid hot-plate of an electric cooker. To prepare a cast iron griddle, heat it well, rub with salt and kitchen paper, remove salt and reheat it slowly and thoroughly for 15 minutes. Before cooking the scones, lightly grease the griddle with a little lard or cooking oil. A griddle with a non-stick surface is ideal and requires no special treatment.

225 g (8 oz) plain flour
5 ml (1 level tsp) bicarbonate of soda
10 ml (2 level tsp) cream of tartar
5 ml (1 level tsp) salt
small knob of lard or margarine
25 g (1 oz) sugar
about 150 ml ($\frac{1}{4}$ pint) milk

Heat then grease a griddle, hot-plate or heavy frying pan. Sift together the dry ingredients, rub in the fat and add the sugar. Mix to a soft but manageable dough with the milk. Divide the dough into two portions. Lightly knead and roll into two flat rounds about 0.5 cm ($\frac{1}{4}$ in) thick. Cut each round into six even triangles and cook on the griddle until evenly brown on one side; turn them and cook on the second side. Allow 5 minutes on each side. Cool on a wire rack. Eat Griddle scones while fresh, buttering them lavishly.
MAKES 12

Potato scones

450 g (1 lb) potatoes, peeled and freshly boiled
salt
50 g (2 oz) butter
100 g (4 oz) plain flour

Preheat a frying pan or griddle (*see above*). Pass the cooked potatoes through a sieve, season well with salt, beat in the butter and gradually work in all the flour. Place the dough on a floured surface and knead to a manageable consistency. Roll out to 0.5 cm ($\frac{1}{4}$ in) thickness and stamp into 6.5-cm (2$\frac{1}{2}$-in) rounds. Cook on the preheated greased griddle or frying pan for about 5 minutes, turning once, until golden brown on both sides.

MAKES 8–12

Scotch pancakes

100 g (4 oz) self-raising flour
15–25 g (½–1 oz) sugar
1 egg
about 150 ml (¼ pint) milk

Preheat a griddle (*see page 51*). Put the flour and sugar in a bowl, add the egg and half the milk and beat until smooth. Add the remaining milk and beat until bubbles rise to the surface. Drop the mixture on to the surface in small rounds from the end of a dessertspoon, spacing well. When bubbles rise on the surface, turn the scones with a palette knife and cook for a further ½–1 minute, or until golden brown. Place inside a clean tea towel over a wire rack while the rest are cooking. Serve buttered.

MAKES ABOUT 15

Rich drop scones

225 g (8 oz) plain flour
10 ml (2 level tsp) cream of tartar
5 ml (1 level tsp) bicarbonate of soda
5 ml (1 level tsp) salt
10 ml (2 level tsp) golden syrup
10 ml (2 level tsp) caster sugar
1 egg
about 300 ml (½ pint) milk

Preheat a griddle (*see page 51*). Sift together the dry ingredients. Add the syrup, sugar and egg and gradually beat in the milk to give a thick batter. Spoon the mixture on to the griddle in small rounds. When bubbles start to burst and the undersides are golden, turn the scones over and cook on the second side; allow about 5 minutes altogether. Place them inside a clean tea towel over a wire cake rack. Serve fresh and warm with butter.

MAKES ABOUT 24

Welsh cakes

225 g (8 oz) plain flour
5 ml (1 level tsp) baking powder
pinch of salt
50 g (2 oz) butter or block margarine
50 g (2 oz) lard
75 g (3 oz) sugar
50 g (2 oz) currants
1 egg, beaten
about 30 ml (2 tbsp) milk

Preheat a griddle (*see page 51*). Sift together the flour, baking powder and salt. Rub in the fats and add the sugar and currants. Bind with egg and milk to give a stiff paste similar to shortcrust pastry. Roll out to 0.5 cm (¼ in) in thickness and cut out with a 7.5-cm (3-in) cutter. Cook the cakes slowly on the griddle for about 3 minutes on each side, until golden brown. Cool on a wire rack. Eat while fresh;

SCOTCH PANCAKES

*Turning pancakes with
a palette knife*

if you like, toss them in caster sugar before leaving them to cool.
MAKES ABOUT 16

Scottish oatcakes

100 g (4 oz) fine oatmeal
pinch of salt
pinch of bicarbonate of soda
small knob of lard, melted
hot water to mix
oatmeal for rolling out

Preheat a griddle (*see page 51*). Place the oatmeal in a basin with the salt and bicarbonate of soda. Make a well in the centre and stir in the lard and enough hot water to make a stiff paste. Roll it out thinly into a large round, using more oatmeal if necessary to prevent it sticking. Cut into four or six wedges. Bake on a moderately hot griddle until they begin to curl at the edges. Turn them over and continue to bake until they are pale brown – or finish browning under the grill. Serve buttered, either with marmalade or honey, or with cheese.

Batch cake

225 g (8 oz) plain flour
10 ml (2 level tsp) baking powder
50 g (2 oz) block margarine
25 g (1 oz) lard
75 g (3 oz) demerara sugar
50 g (2 oz) sultanas
25 g (1 oz) seedless raisins
25 g (1 oz) chopped mixed peel
grated rind of $\frac{1}{2}$ orange
1 large egg
60 ml (4 tbsp) milk

Grease two baking sheets. Sift the flour and baking powder into a bowl and rub in the fats. Stir in sugar, sultanas, raisins and mixed peel. Add the grated orange rind. Beat together the egg and milk and stir into the dry ingredients using a fork. Divide the mixture into two, knead lightly and shape into 15-cm (6-in) rounds about 1 cm ($\frac{1}{2}$ in) thick. Place on the greased baking sheets and bake in the oven at 200°C (400°F) mark 6, for about 25 minutes until pale golden brown. Cool on a wire rack. To serve, split each round in half with a sharp knife, butter and cut into six wedges. The cake should be served whilst still slightly warm.

Date and raisin teabread

100 g (4 oz) butter or block margarine
225 g (8 oz) plain flour
100 g (4 oz) stoned dates, chopped
50 g (2 oz) walnut halves, chopped
100 g (4 oz) seedless raisins
100 g (4 oz) demerara sugar
5 ml (1 level tsp) baking powder
5 ml (1 level tsp) bicarbonate of soda
about 150 ml ($\frac{1}{4}$ pint) milk

Grease and line a loaf tin measuring 25×15 cm ($9\frac{3}{4} \times 5\frac{3}{4}$ in). Rub the fat into the sifted flour until it resembles fine breadcrumbs. Stir in the dates, walnuts, raisins and sugar. Mix the baking powder, bicarbonate of soda and milk in a measure and pour into the centre of the dry ingredients; mix well together to give a stiff dropping consistency. Turn the mixture into the prepared tin and bake in the oven at 180°C (350°F) mark 4, for about 1 hour, until well risen and just firm to the touch. Turn out and cool on a wire rack.

Banana teabread

200 g (7 oz) self-raising flour
1.25 ml ($\frac{1}{4}$ level tsp) bicarbonate of soda
2.5 ml ($\frac{1}{2}$ level tsp) salt
75 g (3 oz) butter or block margarine
175 g (6 oz) sugar
2 eggs, beaten
450 g (1 lb) bananas, mashed
100 g (4 oz) nuts, coarsely chopped

Grease and line an oblong loaf tin, about 21.5×11.5 cm ($8\frac{1}{2} \times 4\frac{1}{2}$ in) top measurements. Sift the flour, bicarbonate of soda and salt. Cream the fat and sugar until pale and fluffy and add the eggs, a little at a time, beating well after each addition. Add the bananas and beat again. Stir in the flour and the nuts. Put into the prepared tin and bake in the oven at 180°C (350°F) mark 4, for about $1\frac{1}{4}$ hours, until well risen and just firm. Turn out and cool on a wire rack. Keep for 24 hours before serving, sliced and buttered.

Honey and banana teabread
Try this variation of the Banana teabread recipe: Reduce the amount of sugar used to 100 g (4 oz) and the bananas to 225 g (8 oz). Beat 30 ml (2 level tbsp) honey into the creamed mixture and add 225 g (8 oz) mixed dried fruits before putting the mixture into the prepared tin.

Cranberry nut bread

Fresh, frozen or drained canned cranberries can be used in this recipe, with equally good results.

225 g (8 oz) plain flour
7.5 ml (1½ level tsp) baking powder
2.5 ml (½ level tsp) bicarbonate of soda
5 ml (1 level tsp) salt
50 g (2 oz) butter or block margarine
175 g (6 oz) sugar
150 ml (¼ pint) orange juice
15 ml (1 tbsp) grated orange rind
1 egg, beaten
75 g (3 oz) walnuts, chopped
100 g (4 oz) cranberries, chopped

Grease and line an oblong loaf tin about 21.5 × 11.5 cm (8½ × 4½ in) top measurements. Sift well together the flour, baking powder, bicarbonate of soda and salt. Rub in the fat and add the sugar. Mix the orange juice, grated rind and beaten egg. Pour into the dry ingredients and mix lightly. Fold in the walnuts and cranberries. Turn into the tin and bake in the oven at 180°C (350°F) mark 4, for 1–1½ hours until risen, golden brown and firm to the touch. Turn out and cool on a wire rack. Keep for 24 hours before serving, thickly sliced and buttered.

Nutty cheese teabread

225 g (8 oz) carton of cottage cheese
175 g (6 oz) soft, dark brown sugar
15 ml (3 level tsp) baking powder
150 g (5 oz) plain flour
3 eggs, beaten
75 g (3 oz) ground almonds
grated rind of 1 orange
100 g (4 oz) walnut halves

For the glaze
golden syrup

Grease and line with greaseproof paper a loaf tin measuring 25.5 × 15 × 7.5 cm (10 × 6 × 3 in). Cream together the cheese and sugar. Sift together the baking powder and flour and add to the creamed mixture alternately with the eggs. Stir in the ground almonds, orange rind and half the walnuts, chopped. Turn the mixture into the prepared tin, level the surface and top with the remainder of the halved walnuts. Bake in the oven at 180°C (350°F) mark 4, for about 1 hour 20 minutes. Cool for 10 minutes in the tin. Turn out and remove the paper straight

away. Brush the top with golden syrup while it is still warm. Cool on a wire rack.

Apple and walnut teabread

100 g (4 oz) butter or block margarine
100 g (4 oz) caster sugar
2 large eggs
15 ml (1 tbsp) honey or golden syrup
100 g (4 oz) sultanas
50 g (2 oz) walnuts, chopped
225 g (8 oz) self-raising flour
pinch of salt
5 ml (1 level tsp) ground mixed spice
1 medium cooking apple, peeled, cored and
   chopped
icing sugar

Grease and line an oblong loaf tin about 21.5 × 11.5 cm (8½ × 4½ in) top measurements. Sift well at room temperature. Place all the ingredients except the icing sugar in a large deep bowl and beat with a wooden spoon until well combined – about 2 minutes. Turn into the prepared tin and level the surface. Bake in the oven at 180°C (350°F) mark 4, for 1 hour. Reduce the oven temperature to 170°C (325°F) mark 3 for about a further 20 minutes. Turn out and cool on a wire rack. When cold, dredge with icing sugar. Serve thickly sliced and buttered.

Apricot tea loaf

225 g (8 oz) dried apricots
300 ml (½ pint) water, less 30 ml (2 tbsp)
175 g (6 oz) caster sugar
75 g (3 oz) lard
2.5 ml (½ level tsp) powdered cinnamon
2.5 ml (½ level tsp) powdered cloves
1.25 ml (¼ level tsp) powdered nutmeg
2.5 ml (½ level tsp) salt
225 g (8 oz) plain flour
5 ml (1 level tsp) bicarbonate of soda
2 eggs, beaten

Grease a loaf tin measuring 23 × 12.5 × 6.5 cm (9 × 5 × 2½ in). Cut the apricots into small pieces and place in a pan with the water, sugar, lard, spices and salt. Simmer for 5 minutes, then leave until cold. Sift together the flour and bicarbonate of soda. Make a well in the centre, stir in the apricot mixture and beaten eggs, mix well, then pour into the prepared tin. Bake in the oven at 180°C (350°F) mark 4, for about 1–1¼ hours. Cool on a wire rack. Slice thinly and spread with butter to serve.

Marmalade teabread

225 g (8 oz) plain flour
7.5 ml (1½ level tsp) baking powder
2.5 ml (½ level tsp) bicarbonate of soda
5 ml (1 level tsp) salt
50 g (2 oz) block margarine
100 g (4 oz) demerara sugar
150 ml (¼ pint) milk
1 egg, beaten
60 ml (4 level tbsp) marmalade
150 g (5 oz) seedless raisins
50 g (2 oz) chopped walnuts

Grease and line a loaf tin with 23 × 11.5 cm (9 × 4½ in) top measurements. Sift together the flour, baking powder, bicarbonate of soda and salt. Rub in the margarine and add the sugar. Combine the milk, beaten egg and marmalade and stir lightly into the flour, followed by the raisins and walnuts. Turn the mixture into the prepared tin, level and bake in the oven at 180°C (350°F) mark 4, for about 1¼ hours. Cool for 10 minutes in the tin, turn out and cool on a wire rack. Serve thickly sliced and buttered.

Marmalade mace teabread

COLOUR PLATE PAGE 49

225 g (8 oz) self-raising flour
pinch of salt
2.5 ml (½ level tsp) ground mace
125 g (4 oz) butter or block margarine
125 g (4 oz) demerara sugar
1 egg, beaten
90 ml (6 level tbsp) chunky marmarlade
60 ml (4 tbsp) milk
3 crystallised orange slices, optional

Grease and line a loaf tin measuring 24 × 13.5 cm (9½ × 5½ in) top measurements. Sift flour, salt and mace together into a basin. Rub in the fat until the mixture resembles fine breadcrumbs. Add the demerara sugar. Stir in the egg, 60 ml (4 level tbsp) marmalade and the milk. Turn the mixture into the prepared cake tin, level the surface and top with the halved slices of orange.

Bake in the oven at 180°C (350°F) mark 4, for about 1 hour. Turn out on to a wire rack. Whilst still warm, brush surface of cake with remaining marmalade. Cool. If wrapped in foil, this teabread stores well for up to a week.

Orange teabread

This is delicious served sliced and spread with honey and cream cheese spread or butter.

50 g (2 oz) butter
175 g (6 oz) caster sugar
1 egg, beaten
grated rind of ½ orange
30 ml (2 tbsp) orange juice
30 ml (2 tbsp) milk
225 g (8 oz) plain flour
12.5 ml (2½ level tsp) baking powder
pinch of salt

Grease and base line a loaf tin measuring 20.5 × 10.5 × 5.5 cm (8 × 4½ × 2¼ in). Beat butter until light, add sugar and beat again until well mixed. Gradually beat in egg until the mixture is smooth and creamy. Slowly add the orange rind and juice : do not worry if the mixture curdles. Lightly beat in the milk alternately with sifted flour, baking powder and salt. Turn into the prepared tin and bake in the oven at 190°C (375°F) mark 5, for 40–50 minutes. Turn out and cool on a wire rack.

Honey teabread

50 g (2 oz) butter or block margarine
150 g (5 oz) honey
150 g (5 oz) demerara sugar
275 g (10 oz) plain flour
pinch of salt
5 ml (1 level tsp) bicarbonate of soda
5 ml (1 level tsp) baking powder
5 ml (1 level tsp) ground mixed spice
5 ml (1 level tsp) ground ginger
5 ml (1 level tsp) powdered cinnamon
50–100 g (2–4 oz) finely chopped mixed peel
1 egg
150 ml (¼ pint) milk
flaked almonds to decorate

Grease and line a loaf tin with 21.5 × 10 cm (8½ × 4 in) top measurements. Gently melt the fat in a pan. Remove from heat, stir in honey and sugar. Leave to cool. Sift flour, salt, raising agents and spices into a bowl. Add the chopped peel. Beat egg and milk together and mix thoroughly with the cooled honey mixture. Pour into the sifted flour etc and beat until smooth. Pour the mixture into the prepared tin and scatter flaked almonds over it. Bake in the oven at 180°C (350°F) mark 4, for 1¼ hours until well risen and firm. Turn out and cool on a wire rack. Keep for 24 hours before serving sliced and buttered.

Raisin malt loaf

225 g (8 oz) plain flour
1.25 ml (¼ level tsp) salt
30 ml (2 level tbsp) soft brown sugar
5 ml (1 level tsp) bicarbonate of soda
150 g (5 oz) seedless raisins
50 g (2 oz) golden syrup
30 ml (2 level tbsp) malt
about 150 ml (¼ pint) milk

Grease and line an oblong loaf tin about 21.5 × 11.5 cm (8½ × 4½ in), top measurements. Sift together the flour, salt, sugar and bicarbonate of soda; add the raisins. Melt the syrup and malt in half of the milk. Make a well in the centre of the dry ingredients, adding more milk to give a sticky, stiff consistency. Put into the tin and bake in the oven at 170°C (325°F) mark 3, for 1–1¼ hours. Turn out to cool on a wire rack and keep for 24 hours before serving, sliced and buttered.

Peanut and orange teabread

226-g (8-oz) jar chunky peanut butter
50 g (2 oz) butter or margarine, softened
225 g (8 oz) self-raising flour
1.25 ml (¼ level tsp) salt
100 g (4 oz) caster sugar
2 eggs
rind and juice of 1 orange
milk
50 g (2 oz) salted peanuts

Grease a loaf tin with 24 × 14 cm (9½ × 5½ in) top measurements. In a large, deep bowl place peanut butter, fat, flour, salt, sugar, eggs and grated orange rind. Squeeze juice from orange and make up to 225 ml (8 fl oz) with milk. Add to bowl and beat all together with a wooden spoon for about 3 minutes. Turn into the prepared loaf tin. Level surface, sprinkle with peanuts, press in lightly. Bake in the oven at 180°C (350°F) mark 4, for about 1¼ hours.

Leave in tin for 10 minutes before turning out to cool on a wire rack. To serve, spread with soft butter before slicing thickly.

Apricot almond teabread

100 g (4 oz) dried apricots
boiling water
225 g (8 oz) self-raising flour
2.5 ml (½ level tsp) salt
75 g (3 oz) caster sugar
40 g (1½ oz) nibbed almonds
grated rind of 1 lemon
1 large egg
100 ml (4 fl oz) milk
40 g (1½ oz) butter, melted

Grease and line a 1.4-litre (2½-pint) loaf tin. Snip apricots into small pieces with scissors. Cover with boiling water and leave to cool. Drain well. Sift together flour and salt and stir in sugar, prepared apricots, almonds and grated lemon rind. Make a well in the centre, pour in blended mixture of eggs, milk and butter and stir into the flour to give a fairly soft dough. Turn into the prepared tin and bake in the oven at 170°C (325°F) mark 3, for about 1½ hours. Turn out on to a wire rack and cool. Serve sliced and spread thickly with butter.

Bran teabread

75 g (3 oz) All-bran
225 g (8 oz) sultanas
225 g (8 oz) soft brown sugar
300 ml (½ pint) milk
175 g (6 oz) self-raising flour
5 ml (1 level tsp) baking powder

Place the bran, sultanas and sugar in a bowl, pour the milk over and leave overnight to soak. The next day, grease and line a loaf tin measuring about 21.5 × 11.5 cm (8½ × 4½ in) top measurements. Sift the flour with the baking powder and stir into the bran mixture. Stir well and turn the mixture into the prepared tin. Bake in the oven at 190°C (375°F) mark 5, for 1–1¼ hours. Turn out the loaf, remove the paper and cool the bread on a wire rack. Serve sliced and buttered.

Family Cakes

A cake for all occasions – that's what you'll find in this chapter: a huge range from one-stage cakes to special Sunday ones. You'll be surprised to discover how quick some of them are to make once you know how. With a little practice a Swiss roll, for example, can be made and cooked in next to no time. This is partly because the cake is cooked in a very shallow tin – the cake must be thin and pliable enough to roll – and partly because the success of rolling it up depends on speedy operation the minute it's out of the oven. This is one recipe it really is worth knowing exactly what to do before you do it rather than following each stage step by step.

Other recipes you will find particularly quick and simple to make are the 'all-in-one' or 'one-stage' cakes: all you have to do is gather the ingredients together, mix them and cook according to instructions. Nothing could be simpler than that!

To make our every occasion cakes a bit more festive we've included a number of icings and fillings. Cover a plain chocolate sponge with Rich chocolate glacé icing, for example, and you've got the perfect birthday cake for a small child's birthday party. Pipe on the child's name and age in plain glacé icing to complete the decoration. Alternatively, if you wish to try your hand at a more elaborate decoration, turn to the chapter on Celebration cakes (page 104) and look particularly at the section entitled 'All about piping'. There are lots of different ideas to choose from and you don't have to be an expert to carry them out.

Each recipe has precise instructions, but you'll find our baking know-how chapter at the back of the book especially helpful to remind you of various skills such as lining cake tins, testing to see if the cake is done and so on. And in the very unlikely event of a mistake, the 'What went wrong' section will help you do even better next time.

Victoria sandwich cake

100 g (4 oz) butter or block margarine
100 g (4 oz) caster sugar
2 eggs, beaten
100 g (4 oz) self-raising flour
30 ml (2 tbsp) jam
caster sugar to dredge

Grease two 18-cm (7-in) sandwich tins and line the base of each with a round of greased greaseproof paper. Cream the fat and sugar until pale and fluffy. Add the egg a little at a time, beating well after each addition. Lightly beat in by hand half the flour, using a wooden spoon, then lightly beat in the rest. Place half the mixture in each tin and level it with a knife. Bake both cakes on the same shelf of the oven at 190°C (375°F) mark 5, for about 20 minutes, or until they are well risen, golden, firm to the touch and beginning to shrink away from the sides of the tins. Turn on to a wire rack to cool. When cakes are cool, sandwich with jam and sprinkle top with sugar.

Variations

Chocolate Replace 45 ml (3 level tbsp) of the flour with 45 ml (3 level tbsp) cocoa. Sandwich together with vanilla or chocolate butter cream.

Orange or lemon Add the finely grated rind of 1 orange or 1 lemon to the mixture. Sandwich the cakes together with orange or lemon curd or orange or lemon butter cream. Use some of the juice of the fruit to make Glacé icing (*see page 72*).

Coffee Add 10 ml (2 level tsp) instant coffee dissolved in a little warm water to creamed mixture with the egg.

Walnut add 25 g (1 oz) walnuts, chopped. Sandwich with Coffee butter cream (*see page 71*). Dust with icing sugar.

One-stage sandwich cake

This is a wonderfully quick method to make a cake without rubbing in or creaming the fat first – but you must use a soft tub margarine.

100 g (4 oz) self-raising flour
5 ml (1 level tsp) baking powder
100 g (4 oz) soft tub margarine
100 g (4 oz) caster sugar
2 eggs
jam or lemon curd to fill

Grease two 18-cm (7-in) sandwich tins and line each base with a round of greased greaseproof paper. Sift the flour and baking powder into a large bowl. Add the other ingredients, mix well, then beat for about 2 minutes. Divide the mixture evenly between the tins. Bake in the oven at 170°C (325°F) mark 3, for 25–35 minutes. When cool, sandwich with jam.

Variations

Orange Add the grated rind and juice of 1 orange.

Mocha Sift 30 ml (2 level tbsp) cocoa and 15 ml (1 level tbsp) instant coffee with 75 g (3 oz) flour.

Chocolate, cherry and nut cake Omit 30 ml (2 level tbsp) sugar and add 60 ml (4 level tbsp) grated plain chocolate, 75 g (3 oz) chopped glacé cherries and 30 ml (2 level tbsp) chopped walnuts.

One-stage fruit cake

225 g (8 oz) self-raising flour
10 ml (2 level tsp) mixed spice
5 ml (1 level tsp) baking powder
100 g (4 oz) soft tub margarine
100 g (4 oz) soft brown sugar
225 g (8 oz) dried fruit
2 eggs
30 ml (2 tbsp) milk

Grease an 18-cm (7-in) round cake tin and line the base with a round of greased greaseproof paper. Sift the flour, spice and baking powder into a large bowl, add the rest of the ingredients and beat until thoroughly combined. Put into the tin and bake in the oven at 170°C (325°F) mark 3, for about 1¾ hours. Turn out to cool on a wire rack.

One-stage marmalade cake

100 g (4 oz) self-raising flour
100 g (4 oz) soft tub margarine
100 g (4 oz) caster sugar
2 eggs
15 ml (1 tbsp) hot water
75 ml (5 level tbsp) chunky marmalade

For the icing
100 g (4 oz) icing sugar
water

Grease and line a 20.5-cm (8-in) deep sandwich tin with greaseproof paper cut deep enough to come 2.5 cm (1 in) above the top of the tin. Sift the flour into a basin; add the margarine, caster sugar, eggs, water and 45 ml (3 level tbsp) marmalade. Beat well with a wooden spoon for 2–3 minutes until evenly blended. Turn mixture into the prepared sandwich tin and bake at 180°C (350°F) mark 4, for 35–40 minutes. Turn out and cool on a wire rack. Spread with 30 ml (2 level tbsp) marmalade. Sift icing sugar and blend with a little water to give a coating consistency and spread over cake. Leave to set.

Walnut coffee cake

This cake is made by the convenient 'all-in-one' or 'one-stage' method (see page 114).

100 g (4 oz) soft tub margarine
100 g (4 oz) caster sugar
2 large eggs
50 g (2 oz) shelled walnuts, chopped
15 ml (1 tbsp) coffee essence
100 g (4 oz) self-raising flour
5 ml (1 level tsp) baking powder
walnut halves for decoration

For the coffee filling
225 g (8 oz) icing sugar
75 g (3 oz) soft tub margarine
30 ml (2 tbsp) milk
10 ml (2 tsp) coffee essence

Grease two 18-cm (7-in) straight-sided sandwich tins and base line them with greased greaseproof paper. Place the margarine, sugar, eggs, chopped walnuts and coffee essence in a deep bowl. Sift the flour and baking powder and beat altogether with a wooden spoon until well combined – 2–3 minutes. Divide between the tins, level the surface and bake in the oven at 170°C (325°F) mark 3, for 35–40 minutes. Turn out and cool on a wire rack.

To make the filling, sift the icing sugar into a bowl, add the margarine, milk and coffee essence and beat thoroughly. Sandwich the cake together with some of the filling, top with rest. Decorate with walnuts.

Victoria sandwich cake made with oil

Cakes made using a vegetable oil are very easy to mix and successful. When using oil for making sandwich cakes, it is essential to add extra raising agent or to whip the egg whites until stiff and to fold them into the beaten mixture just before baking. This helps to counteract the heaviness that sometimes occurs when oil is used.

150 g (5 oz) self-raising flour
5 ml (1 level tsp) baking powder
pinch of salt
125 g (4½ oz) caster sugar
105 ml (7 tbsp) vegetable oil
2 eggs
45 ml (2½ tbsp) milk
few drops of vanilla essence
jam

Grease two 18-cm (7-in) sandwich cake tins and line the base of each with greased greaseproof paper. Sift the flour, baking powder and salt into a bowl and stir in the sugar. Add the oil, eggs, milk and essence and stir with a wooden spoon until the mixture is blended, beat until smooth – not less than 2 minutes. Put into the tins and bake in the oven at 180°C (350°F) mark 4, for 35–40 minutes. Turn out to cool on a wire rack. When cold, sandwich together with jam.

Walnut layer cake

175 g (6 oz) plain flour
2.5 ml (½ level tsp) salt
10 ml (2 level tsp) baking powder
100 g (4 oz) caster sugar
40 g (1½ oz) walnut halves, chopped
2 eggs, separated
75 ml (3 fl oz) vegetable oil
100 ml (4 fl oz) water
5 ml (1 tsp) coffee essence
few walnut halves to decorate

For the filling
100 g (4 oz) icing sugar
50 g (2 oz) butter, softened
5 ml (1 tsp) coffee essence
25 g (1 oz) walnut halves, chopped

For the icing
5 ml (1 tsp) coffee essence
75 g (3 oz) icing sugar
water to mix

Grease and base line two 18-cm (7-in) straight-sided sandwich tins. Sift together the flour, salt and baking powder into a bowl. Stir in caster sugar and nuts. Combine egg yolks, oil, water and essence. Stir into dry ingredients; mix well. Stiffly whisk egg whites and fold into mixture. Divide mixture equally between tins and bake in the oven at 200°C (400°F) mark 6, for about 25 minutes. Remove from tins. Cool on a wire rack.

Sift icing sugar and cream together with butter. Add essence and walnuts. Sandwich cakes together with this filling. Add coffee essence to sifted icing sugar with enough water to make a smooth coating icing. Coat the top of the cake. Decorate with walnut halves.

Fruit cake made with oil

225 g (8 oz) plain flour
10 ml (2 level tsp) baking powder
1.25 ml ($\frac{1}{4}$ level tsp) salt
150 g (5 oz) caster sugar
150 ml ($\frac{1}{4}$ pint) vegetable oil
2 eggs
45–60 ml (3–4 tbsp) milk
275 g (10 oz) mixed dried fruit
100 g (4 oz) glacé cherries, quartered
50 g (2 oz) chopped mixed peel

Grease and line an 18-cm (7-in) cake tin. Sift the flour, baking powder, salt and sugar into a basin. Add the oil, eggs and 45 ml (3 tbsp) milk and beat thoroughly for 2 minutes. Add the dried fruit, cherries and peel and a little more milk if necessary to give a dropping consistency. Put into the tin and bake in the oven at 170°C (325°F) mark 3, for 1 hour, turn down the oven to 150°C (300°F) mark 2, and bake for a further 1$\frac{1}{4}$–1$\frac{1}{2}$ hours. Leave in the tin to cool for 1 hour, then turn it out. When the cake is cold, store it in an airtight tin for at least one day before cutting.

Cherry and orange cake

100 ml (4 fl oz) vegetable oil
2 eggs, beaten
30 ml (2 tbsp) milk
150 g (5 oz) caster sugar
275 g (10 oz) self-raising flour
pinch of salt
225 g (8 oz) glacé cherries, quartered
grated rind of $\frac{1}{2}$ orange

Lightly oil and line an 18-cm (7-in) round cake tin. Whisk together the oil, eggs, milk and sugar. Sift flour and salt, add cherries and grated orange rind. Gradually beat flour mixture into liquid ingredients, using a wooden spoon. Turn mixture into the prepared tin and bake at 180°C (350°F) mark 4 for 1–1$\frac{1}{4}$ hours. Turn out on a wire rack to cool.

Moist coconut cake

This cake is made with oil and may be stored up to one week in an airtight tin.

225 g (8 oz) plain flour
2.5 ml ($\frac{1}{2}$ level tsp) salt
10 ml (2 level tsp) baking powder
15 ml (3 level tsp) ground ginger
25 g (1 oz) desiccated coconut
225 g (8 oz) light soft brown sugar
3 eggs separated
150 ml ($\frac{1}{4}$ pint) vegetable oil
150 ml ($\frac{1}{4}$ pint) milk

Grease and line an 18-cm (7-in) square cake tin. Tie a collar of brown paper round the sides (*see page 116*). Sift together flour, salt, baking powder and ground ginger into a bowl; add coconut and sugar. Stir together beaten egg yolks, oil and milk. Make a well in the centre of the flour, gradually beat in the liquid ingredients, using a wooden spoon. Lastly whisk egg whites until stiff but not dry and fold into 'batter' using a metal spoon. Turn into prepared tin and bake in oven at 170°C (325°F) mark 3, for about 1 hour. Turn out and cool on a wire rack.

Treacle oat squares

This recipe is best stored for a few days in an airtight tin before being cut and served.

100 g (4 oz) self-raising flour
100 g (4 oz) rolled oats
150 ml ($\frac{1}{4}$ pint) vegetable oil
100 g (4 oz) black treacle or golden syrup
100 g (4 oz) demerara sugar
1 egg
60 ml (4 tbsp) milk

Lightly oil and base line a 19-cm (7$\frac{1}{2}$-in) square tin. Put flour and oats into a bowl. Gently warm oil, treacle or syrup and sugar in a pan. Beat egg with the milk. Make a well in the centre of dry ingredients and pour the liquids into it. Beat well for 1–2 minutes, pour into the tin and bake at 170°C (325°F) mark 3, for about 1 hour. Cool on a wire rack and store for a few days before cutting up into squares.

Whisked sponge cake

Whisked mixtures usually contain no fat but a high proportion of eggs and sugar and are made by the whisking method; that is, the eggs and sugar are whisked together and the flour folded in very lightly. They are best eaten the day they are made.

3 large eggs
100 g (4 oz) caster sugar
75 g (3 oz) plain flour

Grease two 18-cm (7-in) sandwich tins and dust with a mixture of a little flour and caster sugar. Put the eggs and sugar in a large deep bowl, stand this over a pan of hot water and whisk until light and creamy – the mixture should be stiff enough to retain the impression of the whisk for a few seconds. (If you are using an electric mixer, no heat is required during whisking.) Remove from the heat and whisk until cool. Sift half the flour over the mixture and fold in very lightly, using a metal spoon. Add the remaining flour in the same way. Pour the mixture into the tins and bake in the oven at 190°C (375°F) mark 5, for 20–25 minutes. Turn them out to cool on a wire rack.

Sponge fingers

COLOUR PLATE PAGE 64

75 ml (5 level tbsp) plain flour
75 ml (5 level tbsp) caster sugar
1 large egg

Grease a sponge finger tray and dust with 15 ml (1 level tbsp) flour and 15 ml (1 level tbsp) sugar. Put the egg and remaining sugar in a deep bowl and (unless you are using an electric mixer) stand this over hot water; whisk until light, creamy and stiff enough to retain the impression of the whisk for a few seconds. Remove from the heat and whisk until cool. Sift half the remaining flour over the mixture and fold in very lightly, using a metal spoon. Add the remaining flour in the same way. Spoon just enough mixture into each hollow in the tray to reach the top. Bake in the oven at 200°C (400°F) mark 6, for about 10 minutes, until golden. Remove sponge fingers carefully from the tray and cool on a wire rack. Eat on day of making.
MAKES 12

Variation
Dip the ends of the fingers into melted chocolate and allow to harden.

Sponge drops

COLOUR PLATE PAGE 64

Grease a baking sheet, or line it with non-stick paper. Make the mixture as for sponge fingers and spoon or pipe small rounds using a 2.5-cm (½-in)

plain nozzle, on to the sheet, fairly far apart. Bake in the oven for 8–10 minutes, until golden. Remove from the sheet and cool. When cold, dust with icing sugar, sandwich in pairs with whipped cream, or dip one side of each drop in melted chocolate.
MAKES 6 PAIRS

Chocolate layer cake

100 g (4 oz) butter or block margarine
100 g (4 oz) caster sugar
2 large eggs
15 g (½ oz) cocoa
100 g (4 oz) self-raising flour
apricot jam, sieved
75 g (3 oz) plain chocolate cake covering

For the filling
40 g (1½ oz) butter
75 g (3 oz) icing sugar
10 ml (2 tsp) coffee essence
15 ml (1 tbsp) top of milk

Grease and line a straight-sided 20.5-cm (8-in) sandwich tin and line with greaseproof paper to come 2.5 cm (1 in) above tin. Cream the fat and beat in the sugar until the mixture is light and fluffy. Beat in the eggs one at a time. Blend the cocoa to a paste with a little water. Lightly beat it into the creamed mixture, alternately with the flour. Turn the mixture into the tin, level and bake in the oven at 180°C (350°F) mark 4, for about 30 minutes. Turn out and cool on a wire rack. Split and sandwich with the coffee filling (made by creaming all the ingredients together). Brush the top with sieved apricot jam. Melt the chocolate in a bowl over a pan of hot water and spread over the jam. When set but not firm, mark the icing into eight portions.

Fudge cake

225 g (8 oz) butter or block margarine
225 g (8 oz) soft dark brown sugar
4 large eggs
20 ml (4 tsp) coffee essence
225 g (8 oz) self-raising flour
apricot jam, sieved
50 g (2 oz) walnuts, finely chopped
icing sugar

For the chocolate butter cream
100 g (4 oz) butter
100 g (4 oz) icing sugar
60 ml (4 level tbsp) cocoa
60–90 ml (4–6 tbsp) top of milk

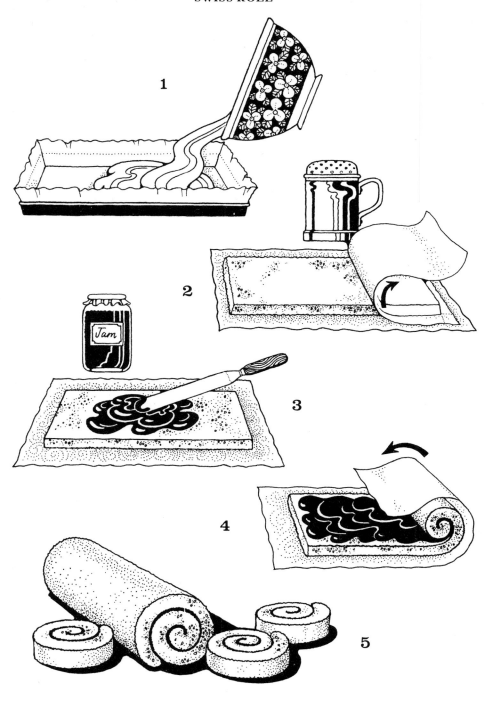

1   Pouring the mixture into the prepared tin
2   Quickly turning the sponge on to sugared paper
3   Spreading with jam once the edges have been trimmed
4   Rolling up the Swiss roll
5   Finished Swiss roll

Grease two 20.5-cm (8-in) sandwich tins and line with greaseproof paper to come 2.5 cm (1 in) above tins. Beat the fat until soft and creamy, add the brown sugar and continue to cream until light, fluffy and pale in colour. Beat in the eggs one at a time. Lightly beat in the coffee essence and the flour. Divide the mixture between the tins and level the tops. Bake in the oven at 190°C (375°F) mark 5, until well risen and spongy to the touch – about 30 minutes. Turn out and cool on a wire rack. When cold, sandwich the layers together with jam.

Spread the sides of the cake with a little of the chocolate butter cream (see below) and roll them in chopped nuts. Dredge the top heavily with icing sugar and mark into eight sections with the back of a knife. Put the remaining butter cream into a forcing bag fitted with a star nozzle and use to decorate the cake (*see page 109*).

To make Chocolate butter cream: Cream the butter, sift in the icing sugar and beat until fluffy. Add the sifted cocoa and enough milk to give a piping consistency beating after each addition.

Swiss roll

COLOUR PLATE PAGE 64

3 large eggs
100 g (4 oz) caster sugar
100 g (4 oz) plain flour
15 ml (1 tbsp) hot water
caster sugar to dredge
warm jam

Line a Swiss roll tin 33.6 × 22.5 cm (13 × 9 in). Put the eggs and sugar in a large deep bowl, stand it over a pan of hot water and whisk until thick, light and creamy: the mixture should be stiff enough to retain the impression of the whisk for a few seconds. Remove the bowl from the heat and whisk until cool. (If you are using an electric mixer, no heat is required during the whisking.) Sift half the flour over the mixture and fold in very lightly, using a metal spoon. Add the remaining flour in the same way and lightly stir in the hot water. Pour the mixture into the prepared tin, tilt the tin backwards and forwards allowing it to run over the whole surface. Bake in the oven at 220°C (425°F) mark 7, for 7–9 minutes until golden-brown, well risen and spongy.

Meanwhile, have ready a sheet of greaseproof paper liberally sprinkled with caster sugar. To help make the sponge pliable, you can place the paper over a tea towel lightly wrung out in hot water. Turn the cake quickly out on to the paper, trim off the crusty

edges with a sharp knife and spread the surface with warmed jam. Roll up quickly with the aid of the paper, making the first turn firmly so that the whole cake will roll evenly and have a good shape when finished, but roll more lightly after this first turn. Dredge the cake with sugar and cool on a wire rack.

Chocolate Swiss roll
Replace 15 ml (1 level tbsp) of the flour with 15 ml (1 level tbsp) cocoa. If you are using a cream filling, turn out the cooked sponge and trim as above, but do not spread with the filling immediately. Roll the sponge up loosely with the sheet of greaseproof paper inside. When the cake is cold, unroll, remove paper, spread with cream or Butter cream (*see page 71*) and re-roll.

Small Swiss rolls
Bake a sponge as above. When it is cooked, turn it out, trim and cut in half lengthways. Spread each half with jam and roll up, starting at the longer sides and making two long thin rolls. When the cake is cold, cut each roll into three even lengths. Other fillings may be used, or the rolls may be coated with glacé icing.

Sunday chocolate cake

75 g (3 oz) plain block chocolate
180 ml (12 tbsp) milk
75 g (3 oz) butter
175 g (6 oz) plain flour
10 ml (2 level tsp) baking powder
5 ml (1 level tsp) bicarbonate of soda
75 g (3 oz) caster sugar
1 egg
vanilla essence

For the frosting
100 g (4 oz) butter
50 g (2 oz) cocoa powder
50 g (2 oz) caster sugar
50 g (2 oz) icing sugar
vanilla essence
30 ml (2 tbsp) double cream (optional)

Grease a 22-cm (8½-in) straight-sided sandwich tin and line with a band of greaseproof paper to come 2.5 cm (1 in) above the edge of the tin. In a small pan put the broken chocolate, milk and butter, and heat without boiling, stirring until the chocolate is thoroughly blended. Cool for 5 minutes.

Sift the flour, baking powder and bicarbonate of soda together in a bowl, add the sugar. Pour on the chocolate mixture, add the egg and vanilla essence, and beat with a rotary or wire whisk until smooth. Pour into the prepared tin. Bake in the oven at 180°C (350°F) mark 4, for about 35 minutes until well-risen and just firm. Turn out and cool on a wire rack. Store in an airtight tin for a few days if wished. Cover the top before serving with chocolate cream frosting.

To make the frosting, cream the butter and beat in the sifted cocoa, caster sugar and icing sugar. Add a few drops of vanilla essence and, if used, beat in the double cream.

Gingerbread

350 g (12 oz) plain flour
pinch of salt
5 ml (1 level tsp) ground cinnamon
10 ml (2 level tsp) ground ginger
5 ml (1 level tsp) bicarbonate of soda
100 g (4 oz) butter or block margarine
100 g (4 oz) sugar
grated rind and juice of 1 orange
75 g (3 oz) chopped mixed peel
100 g (4 oz) treacle, warmed
2 eggs, beaten
little milk if necessary

Grease and line an 18-cm (7-in) square cake tin. Sift the flour, salt, spices and bicarbonate of soda and rub in the fat until the mixture resembles fine bread-crumbs. Stir in the sugar, orange rind and juice, chopped peel, treacle and eggs; mix to a pouring consistency, adding a little milk if necessary. Put into the tin and bake in the oven at 170°C (325°F) mark 3, for about 1¼ hours. Turn out to cool on a wire rack.

Light fruit cake

175 g (6 oz) butter or block margarine
175 g (6 oz) caster sugar
3 eggs
125 g (4 oz) plain flour
150 g (5 oz) self-raising flour
50 g (2 oz) glacé cherries, halved
225 g (8 oz) mixed dried fruit
grated rind and juice of ½ lemon
walnut halves
15 ml (1 level tbsp) granulated sugar

Grease and line an 18-cm (7-in) round cake tin. Cream the fat, add sugar and continue creaming until light and fluffy. Beat in eggs one at a time. Combine flours, cherries and mixed dried fruit. Fold into the creamed mixture alternately with the lemon rind and the juice.

Turn mixture into the prepared cake tin, level the surface. Top with halved walnuts, sprinkle with granulated sugar and bake in the oven at 170°C (325°F) mark 3, for about 1 hour 40 minutes until firm to the touch. Turn out and cool on a wire rack.

Half-pound cake

225 g (8 oz) butter or block margarine
225 g (8 oz) caster sugar
4 eggs, beaten
225 g (8 oz) seedless raisins
225 g (8 oz) mixed currants and sultanas
100 g (4 oz) glacé cherries, halved
225 g (8 oz) plain flour
2.5 ml (½ level tsp) salt
2.5 ml (½ level tsp) mixed spice
60 ml (4 tbsp) brandy or milk
few halved walnuts

Line a 20.5-cm (8-in) round cake tin with double greased greaseproof paper. Cream the fat and sugar together until pale and fluffy. Add the eggs a little at a time, beating well after each addition. Mix the fruit, flour, salt and spice and fold into the creamed mixture, using a metal spoon. Add the brandy or milk and mix to a soft dropping consistency. Put the mixture in the tin, level the top and put on the nuts. Bake in the oven at 150°C (300°F) mark 2, for about 2½ hours. Turn out to cool on a wire rack.

Farmhouse cake

225 g (8 oz) wholemeal flour
225 g (8 oz) plain flour
5 ml (1 level tsp) mixed spice
5 ml (1 level tsp) bicarbonate of soda
175 g (6 oz) butter or block margarine
225 g (8 oz) sugar
100 g (4 oz) sultanas
100 g (4 oz) raisins, stoned
45 ml (3 level tbsp) chopped mixed peel
1 egg, beaten
300 ml (½ pint) milk

Grease and flour a 20.5-cm (8-in) tin. Sift the flours, spice and bicarbonate of soda. Rub the fat into the dry ingredients until the mixture resembles fine bread-crumbs. Stir in the sugar, fruit and peel. Make a well in the centre, pour in the egg and some of the milk and gradually work in the dry ingredients, adding more milk if necessary to give a dropping consistency; put the mixture into the tin and level the top. Bake in the

oven at 170°C (325°F) mark 3, for about 2 hours, until firm to the touch. Turn out and cool on a wire rack.

Genoa cake

75 g (3 oz) Brazil nuts, shelled
100 g (4 oz) glacé cherries, quartered
100 g (4 oz) chopped mixed peel
225 g (8 oz) sultanas
10 ml (2 level tsp) baking powder
350 g (12 oz) plain flour
grated rind and juice of 1 lemon
225 g (8 oz) butter or block margarine
225 g (8 oz) caster sugar
3 large eggs, beaten

Grease and line a 20.5-cm (8-in) square cake tin. Roughly chop 50 g (2 oz) nuts and pare the remainder in thin slices for decoration. Mix together the chopped nuts, cherries, peel and sultanas. Sift together the baking powder and flour and add the lemon rind. Cream together the fat and sugar until light and fluffy. Gradually beat in the eggs. Fold in the flour and lemon juice and lastly add the fruit. Turn the mixture into the tin, level the surface and sprinkle with the sliced nuts. Bake in the oven at 190°C (375°F) mark 5, for 1–1¼ hours. Cool on a rack. Serve cut in squares.

Bishop's cake

Follow the above recipe, but replace the Brazil nuts, sultanas and lemon by 50 g (2 oz) walnuts or almonds, chopped, and 50 g (2 oz) angelica, chopped; replace the 350 g (12 oz) flour by 275 g (10 oz) plain flour and 50 g (2 oz) ground almonds. Slice thickly to serve.

Ginger loaf cake

175 g (6 oz) butter
75 g (3 oz) soft brown sugar
75 g (3 oz) golden syrup
3 eggs
225 g (8 oz) self-raising flour
10–20 ml (2–4 level tsp) ground ginger
4 pieces of stem ginger, finely chopped
25 g (1 oz) flaked almonds

Grease and base line a loaf tin with 23 × 12.5 cm (9 × 5 in) top measurements. Cream butter, add sugar and syrup and continue creaming until the mixture is light and fluffy. Add eggs, one at a time,

beating well. Sift together the flour and ginger and fold into creamed mixture. Fold in chopped ginger. Turn mixture into prepared loaf tin. Sprinkle flaked almonds over the mixture, press in lightly and bake in the oven at 180°C (350°F) mark 4, for about 1 hour 10 minutes, until risen and firm to the touch. Turn out and cool on wire rack.

Almond loaf

50 g (2 oz) ground almonds
275 g (10 oz) Barbados sugar
225 g (8 oz) butter or block margarine
a little beaten egg
225 g (8 oz) butter or block margarine
4 eggs
225 g (8 oz) wholemeal plain flour
10 ml (2 level tsp) baking powder

Grease and line a loaf tin measuring 23 × 12.5 × 6.5 cm (9 × 5 × 2½ in). Make a paste with the ground almonds, 50 g (2 oz) of the sugar and a little beaten egg. Cream together the remaining sugar and the fat until soft and fluffy.

Beat in the eggs, one at a time. Fold in the flour and baking powder sifted together, adding a little milk if necessary to give a soft dropping consistency. Put one third of the cake mixture in the prepared tin and place little pieces of the almond paste over it. Continue to add the cake mixture and almond paste in layers, finishing with the creamed mixture. Bake in the oven at 180°C (350°F) mark 4, for about 1½ hours. Turn out and cool on a wire rack.

Crunchy-top loaf cake

For the topping
50 g (2 oz) plain flour
100 g (4 oz) caster sugar
50 g (2 oz) butter
20 ml (4 level tsp) ground cinnamon

For the base
350 g (12 oz) plain flour
225 g (8 oz) caster sugar
20 ml (4 level tsp) baking powder
pinch of salt
175 g (6 oz) butter or block margarine
grated rind of 1 lemon
2 eggs
175 ml (6 fl oz) milk

Grease and flour a long loaf tin measuring 33 × 11.5 × 6.5 cm (13 × 4½ × 2½ in).

Almond crisps · Grantham gingerbreads · Swiss tarts
Florentines · Macaroons

For the topping, sift the flour into a bowl, add the sugar, rub in the butter and stir in the cinnamon; set aside.

For the base, sift the flour, sugar, baking powder and salt together and rub in the butter or margarine until the mixture resembles fine breadcrumbs. Add the lemon rind. Beat the eggs and milk together, pour on to the dry ingredients and mix to a soft consistency. Turn the base mixture into the prepared tin, sprinkle with the topping and smooth with the back of a spoon. Bake in the oven at 190°C (375°F) mark 5, for about 1 hour. (Cover with foil if it shows signs of over-browning.) Turn out carefully on to a cake rack lined with a clean tea towel, reverse and leave to cool.

Orange peel kugelhupf

225 g (8 oz) butter
225 g (8 oz) caster sugar
3 eggs
225 g (8 oz) self-raising flour
grated rind of 1 orange
50 g (2 oz) finely chopped mixed peel

For the orange syrup
50 g (2 oz) icing sugar
75 ml (5 tbsp) orange juice

Brush a 1.7-litre (3-pint) kugelhupf fancy ring tin with lard. Cream together the butter and sugar until really light and fluffy. Beat in the eggs, one at a time. Gently beat in the sifted flour and then the orange rind

ORANGE PEEL KUGELHUPF

Turning the mixture into a traditional ring tin

and mixed peel. Turn into the ring tin. Place on a baking sheet and bake in the oven at 190°C (375°F) mark 5, for about 1 hour. Turn out and while still hot, spoon over the orange syrup made by blending the orange juice with the sifted icing sugar. Leave until cold, keep for 24 hours before slicing.

Date and nut loaf

350 g (12 oz) plain flour
175 g (6 oz) butter or block margarine
175 g (6 oz) caster sugar
10 ml (2 level tsp) ground cinnamon
175 g (6 oz) chopped mixed nuts and 175 g (6 oz) chopped dates, mixed
411-g (14½-oz) can of apple purée
7.5 ml (1½ level tsp) bicarbonate of soda
15 ml (1 tbsp) milk

For the topping
30 ml (2 level tbsp) dates and nuts, chopped
10 ml (2 level tsp) caster sugar
2.5 ml (½ level tsp) ground cinnamon

Grease and line a loaf tin measuring 25.5 × 15 × 7.5 cm (10 × 6 × 3 in).

Sift the flour into a bowl and rub in the fat; add the sugar, cinnamon, nuts and dates. Make a well in the centre and add the apple purée. Dissolve the bicarbonate of soda in the milk and add to the mixture; mix well and put into the prepared tin. Mix together the ingredients for the topping, sprinkle over the surface and bake in the oven at 190°C (375°F) mark 5, for about 1¼ hours. Carefully remove from the tin when cooked and cool on a wire rack.

Date ripple loaf

225 g (8 oz) cooking apples, peeled and cored
150 g (5 oz) stoned cooking dates
grated rind and juice of 1 lemon
45 ml (3 tbsp) water
125 g (4 oz) butter
125 g (4 oz) dark brown sugar
2 eggs, beaten
125 g (4 oz) self-raising flour

Chop the apples and 125 g (4 oz) dates and place in a saucepan with the lemon rind and juice and water. Cook over a gentle heat until a soft purée. Beat well and cool. Cream together butter and sugar until light and fluffy. Gradually beat in eggs then lightly beat in the flour. Spoon one third of the cake mixture into a non-stick rectangular cake tin with 26.5 × 10 cm

($10\frac{1}{2} \times 4$ in) top measurements and spread mixture over base. On top of this spread half the date mixture. Repeat the layering, finishing with cake mixture. Cut remaining 25 g (1 oz) dates into thin slivers and arrange in a line down the length of the cake. Bake in the oven at 170°C (325°F) mark 3, for about 1 hour 10 minutes. Cover with foil half-way through cooking time. This mixture also fits a greased loaf tin measuring $22 \times 11 \times 6.5$ cm ($8\frac{3}{4} \times 4\frac{3}{8} \times 2\frac{1}{2}$ in).

Date and pineapple loaf

Store this cake for 1–2 days in an airtight tin before cutting.

175 g (6 oz) butter or block margarine
350 g (12 oz) self-raising flour
175 g (6 oz) caster sugar
100 g (4 oz) stoned dates, chopped
100 g (4 oz) glacé pineapple, cut finely
2 eggs
45 ml (3 tbsp) milk
5 ml (1 tsp) pineapple essence
12 cubes lump sugar, crushed

Grease and line a loaf tin with 23.5×14.5 cm ($9\frac{3}{4} \times 5\frac{3}{4}$ in) top measurements. In a bowl rub the fat into the flour, add the caster sugar, dates and pineapple. Beat the eggs, milk and essence together. Pour on to dry ingredients and mix to a soft consistency. Turn into prepared tin, level surface, sprinkle crushed sugar over and bake in the oven at 180°C (350°F) mark 4, for about $1\frac{1}{4}$ hours. Turn out and cool on a wire rack.

Lemon loaf cake

A cake which is good to make and eat whilst fresh – though it does keep and mellow, wrapped in kitchen foil, for two to three days. The very thin lemon glaze is drizzled over the warm cake, making it moist and giving the crust a delicious flavour.

100 g (4 oz) block margarine
175 g (6 oz) caster sugar
2 eggs
grated rind of 1 lemon
175 g (6 oz) self-raising flour

For the glaze
30 ml (2 tbsp) lemon juice
50 g (2 oz) icing sugar, sifted

Line a loaf tin with 21.5×11.5 cm ($8\frac{1}{2} \times 4\frac{1}{2}$ in) top measurements, 1.4-litre ($2\frac{1}{2}$-pint) capacity. Cream together fat and caster sugar by hand. Beat in the eggs, one at a time, together with the grated lemon rind. Lightly beat in the flour. Turn into prepared loaf tin. Level the surface and bake in the oven at 180°C (350°F) mark 4, for 50–60 minutes. A slight dip may form in the centre of the cake but it will not spoil the texture. Turn out upside down on to a wire rack.

Whilst the cake is cooking make the glaze by combining the lemon juice with the icing sugar. Prick the cake all over with a fine skewer and whilst still hot brush evenly all over with the glaze. Reverse and repeat on the top crust until all the glaze is absorbed. Cool on the rack. Serve in thick slices.

Belgian cake

75 g (3 oz) block margarine
100 g (4 oz) caster sugar
1 egg
225 g (8 oz) self-raising flour
105 ml (7 level tbsp) mincemeat
15–30 ml (1–2 tbsp) sherry

Grease an 18-cm (7-in) square cake tin. Cream together the margarine and sugar, then beat in the egg. Stir in the flour and mix well. Spread two thirds of the mixture over the base and up the sides of the greased cake tin. Mix together mincemeat and sherry and spread in prepared tin over creamed mixture. Divide remaining mixture into eight, and roll out into long strips. Place on top of cake in a lattice pattern. Bake in the oven at 180°C (350°F) mark 4, for about 35 minutes. Remove from tin and cool on a wire rack. Sprinkle with icing sugar.

Grasmere cake

350 g (12 oz) plain flour
5 ml (1 level tsp) mixed spice
7.5 ml ($1\frac{1}{2}$ level tsp) bicarbonate of soda
175 g (6 oz) butter or block margarine
175 g (6 oz) demerara sugar
175 g (6 oz) currants
75 g (3 oz) sultanas
a good 300 ml ($\frac{1}{2}$ pint) milk + 15 ml (1 tbsp) lemon juice or a good 300 ml ($\frac{1}{2}$ pint) sour milk

Grease and line a loaf tin measuring $23.5 \times 14.5 \times 7.5$ cm ($9\frac{3}{4} \times 5\frac{3}{4} \times 3$ in). Sift together the flour, spice and bicarbonate of soda. Rub in the fat and add the sugar, currants and sultanas. Sour the milk by adding the lemon juice or, if available, use sour milk. Gradually add sour milk to dry ingredients to give a dropping consistency. Leave, covered, overnight. Next day, turn into prepared tin and bake in the oven at 170°C (325°F) mark 3, for about 2 hours. Turn out of tin and leave to cool on a wire rack.

Raspberry coconut tea cake

1 egg, separated
75 g (3 oz) caster sugar
15 ml (1 tbsp) melted butter
2.5 ml ($\frac{1}{2}$ tsp) vanilla essence
120 ml (8 tbsp) milk
30 ml (2 level tbsp) shredded coconut
175 g (6 oz) self-raising flour
30 ml (2 tbsp) raspberry jam
shredded coconut for topping

Grease and base line an 18-cm (7-in) round cake tin. Whisk egg white until stiff. Add sugar gradually to whisked egg white, beating well. Add yolk, butter, vanilla essence and milk. Stir in coconut and flour. Place two-thirds of the mixture into the prepared cake tin. Dot with jam. Cover with remaining mixture, and sprinkle with extra coconut. Bake in the oven at 190°C (375°F) mark 5, for 30–40 minutes. Turn out and cool on a wire rack.

Orange and pineapple cake

125 g (4 oz) or 175 g (6 oz) glacé pineapple cubes
50 g (2 oz) ground almonds
75 g (3 oz) self-raising flour
75 g (3 oz) plain flour
juice of 1 small orange
175 g (6 oz) butter
175 g (6 oz) caster sugar
3 eggs
apricot jam
50 g (2 oz) icing sugar

Grease and base line a 20.5-cm (8-in), 1.1-litre (2-pint) capacity moule à manqué tin. With a wet sharp knife cut each cube of the 125 g (4 oz) pineapple into four slices. If using 175 g (6 oz) pineapple, finely chop the extra 50 g (2 oz). In a bowl combine almonds, flours, grated rind of the orange and the chopped pineapple if used. Squeeze the juice from the orange. Cream together the butter and sugar until light and fluffy; beat in the eggs one at a time. Fold in the dry ingredients alternately with 30 ml (2 tbsp) of the orange juice. Turn into the prepared moule à manqué tin. Level the surface and bake in the oven at 180°C (350°F) mark 4, for 45–55 minutes until well risen and

spongy to the touch. Turn out on to a wire rack to cool with base uppermost.

Brush the base of the cake with apricot jam. Arrange slices of pineapple over the jam. Blend icing sugar with just enough orange juice or water to give a thin coating consistency. Spoon over the pineapple and leave to set.

Sultana spice cake

225 g (8 oz) butter or block margarine
225 g (8 oz) dark soft brown sugar
4 eggs
225 g (8 oz) self-raising flour
pinch of salt
5 ml (1 level tsp) ground allspice
5 ml (1 level tsp) ground ginger
100 g (4 oz) sultanas
50 g (2 oz) crystallised or stem ginger, chopped
50 g (2 oz) shelled walnuts, chopped

Grease and line a 23 × 18 cm (9 × 7 in) deep cake tin. Cream together the butter and sugar until light and fluffy. Beat in the eggs, one at a time. Sift together the flour, salt and spices, add the fruit and nuts. Fold into the creamed mixture. Turn the mixture into the prepared tin, level the surface and bake in the oven at 170°C (325°F) mark 3, for about 1$\frac{1}{2}$ hours. Cool, remove from tins, allow to go cold on a wire rack.

Raisin cake

450 g (1 lb) stoned raisins
50 g (2 oz) stem ginger
175 g (6 oz) butter
75 g (3 oz) caster sugar
75 g (3 oz) soft brown sugar
2 large eggs
250 g (9 oz) plain flour
7.5 ml (1$\frac{1}{2}$ level tsp) baking powder
45 ml (3 tbsp) orange juice
grated rind of 1 orange
flaked almonds to decorate

Grease and line a 20.5-cm (8-in) round cake tin. Pick over the raisins just in case the odd stone remains, cut large raisins in half. Chop the ginger. Beat the butter until creamy. Add sugars and beat again until light and fluffy. Beat in the eggs one at a time. Sift the flour and baking powder into the creamed ingredients and stir in with the orange juice and rind. Fold in the raisins and ginger. Turn into the tin. Hollow the centre slightly and scatter a few flaked almonds over the surface. Bake in the oven at 180°C (350°F) mark 4, for about 1½–2 hours. After 45 minutes cover with a double thickness of greaseproof or brown paper. Turn out and cool on a wire rack.

Butterscotch cake

100 g (4 oz) butter
175 g (6 oz) soft brown sugar
2 eggs
15 ml (1 tbsp) golden syrup
120 ml (8 tbsp) milk
2.5 ml (½ tsp) vanilla essence
225 g (8 oz) self-raising flour
pinch of salt

For the caramel icing
225 g (8 oz) soft brown sugar
30 ml (2 tbsp) milk
25 g (1 oz) butter

For the decoration
whole nuts (brazils, walnuts, almonds)
clear honey

Grease and line an 18-cm (7-in) square cake tin. Cream together the butter and sugar. Separate the eggs and beat yolks into creamed mixture. Stir in syrup, milk and essence. Sift flour and salt on top of mixture then fold into the mixture. Beat egg whites until stiff, fold gently into the mixture. Put mixture into the prepared cake tin. Bake in the oven at 180°C (350°F) mark 4, for about 1 hour. Remove from tin and cool on a wire rack.

To make the caramel icing, put all the ingredients into a saucepan. Bring slowly to the boil, stirring. Boil gently for 7 minutes, then remove from heat. Beat until creamy. Spread on top of cake with a wetted knife. Place whole nuts around top edge of cake, and brush them with a little clear honey to glaze.

Eggless cake

225 g (8 oz) lard
450 g (1 lb) plain flour
10 ml (2 level tsp) ground ginger
175 g (6 oz) caster sugar
175 g (6 oz) sultanas
175 g (6 oz) currants
10 ml (2 level tsp) bicarbonate of soda
300 ml (½ pint) milk
30 ml (2 tbsp) vinegar

Grease and line a loaf tin measuring 24 × 14 × 7.5 cm (9½ × 5½ × 3 in).* Rub the lard into the sifted flour

and ginger. Add the sugar and fruit. Dissolve the bicarbonate of soda in the milk, add the vinegar and mix quickly into the dry ingredients. Turn the mixture into the tin, make a hollow in the top and bake in the oven at 190°C (375°F) mark 5, for about 2 hours. Turn out on to a wire rack to cool.

Alternatively, use two loaf tins each measuring 21.5 × 11 × 6.5 cm (8⅜ × 4⅜ × 2½ in). In this case reduce the cooking time to about 1¼ hours.

Marmalade cake

350 g (12 oz) self-raising flour
5 ml (1 level tsp) baking powder
pinch of salt
175 g (6 oz) margarine
100 g (4 oz) light soft brown sugar
175 g (6 oz) seedless raisins
grated rind of 1 orange
60 ml (4 tbsp) orange juice
2 large eggs
60 ml (4 tbsp) milk
350 g (12 oz) thick cut marmalade

Grease and line an 18 × 28 cm (7 × 11 in) cake tin. Sift together the flour, baking powder and salt. Rub in the margarine and stir in the sugar and raisins. Add the orange rind and juice. Beat the eggs with 30 ml (2 tbsp) milk, stir into the mixture with more milk to give a soft dropping consistency. Spoon into the prepared tin. Put spoonfuls of marmalade over the mixture, reserving 75 g (3 oz) to glaze. Bake in the oven at 190°C (375°F) mark 5, for about 1 hour. Cool in the tin for 30 minutes and then turn out and cool on a wire rack. Brush with reserved marmalade and leave until cold. Eat fresh, cut into squares.

Peel and nut cake

100 g (4 oz) plain flour
225 g (8 oz) self-raising flour
75 g (3 oz) cornflour
1.25 ml (¼ level tsp) salt
250 g (9 oz) butter
200 g (7½ oz) caster sugar
4 large eggs
grated rind of 1 lemon
10 ml (2 tsp) lemon juice
15 ml (1 tbsp) brandy
90 ml (6 tbsp) milk
225 g (8 oz) finely chopped mixed peel
100 g (4 oz) flaked almonds
granulated sugar

Grease and line a 23-cm (9-in) square cake tin. Sift together flours, cornflour and salt. Cream together butter and sugar, gradually beat in eggs one at a time. Alternately fold in flour with lemon rind and juice, brandy and milk. Fold in the finely chopped mixed peel and the nuts.

Turn mixture into the prepared tin, slightly hollow the centre, sprinkle with a little granulated sugar and bake at 180°C (350°F) mark 4, for about 1¾ hours. Test the centre of the cake with a fine skewer. Turn out and cool on a wire rack.

Grandmother's boiled fruit cake

300 ml (¼ pint) freshly made tea
100 g (4 oz) margarine
150 g (5 oz) light soft brown sugar
175 g (6 oz) currants
175 g (6 oz) sultanas
15 ml (3 level tsp) mixed spice
275 g (10 oz) plain flour
10 ml (2 level tsp) bicarbonate of soda
1 large egg

Grease a round cake tin 18 cm (17 in) in diameter. Put the tea, margarine, sugar, currants, sultanas and spice in a saucepan and bring to the boil, reduce the heat and simmer for 20 minutes. Cool. Lightly beat in the sifted flour and bicarbonate of soda with the egg. Turn the mixture into the tin and bake in the oven at 180°C (350°F) mark 4, for about 1 hour. When the cake is beginning to brown, cover with a piece of greaseproof paper. Turn out and cool on a wire rack.

Old-fashioned plum cake

450 g (1 lb) tenderised prunes
150 g (5 oz) butter
150 g (5 oz) block margarine
275 g (10 oz) caster sugar
grated rind of 1 lemon
5 large eggs
150 g (5 oz) self-raising flour
150 g (5 oz) plain flour
1.25 ml (¼ level tsp) salt
15 ml (1 tbsp) sherry
50 g (2 oz) nibbed almonds
50 g (2 oz) ground almonds

Grease and line a 23.5 × 13 × 7.5 cm (9¼ × 5¼ × 3 in) loaf tin, 2.3-litre (4-pint) capacity. Remove prune flesh from stones and roughly chop. Cream fats and sugar, add lemon rind and beat in eggs one at a time. Lightly beat in sifted flours, salt and sherry. Fold in prepared prunes, nibbed and ground almonds. Turn

into prepared tin, bake in oven at 150°C (300°F) mark 2, for 2½–3 hours. Cool on a wire rack.

Cherry and raisin cake

350 g (12 oz) self-raising flour
pinch of salt
175 g (6 oz) margarine
175 g (6 oz) glacé cherries
100 g (4 oz) stoned raisins
50 g (2 oz) desiccated coconut
175 g (6 oz) caster sugar
2 large eggs
approx 150 ml (¼ pint) milk

Grease a 19 × 20.5 cm (7½ × 8 in) round cake tin. Sift the flour and salt into a bowl. Rub in the margarine until the mixture resembles fine breadcrumbs. Halve the cherries and raisins using scissors. Toss in the coconut and add to the dry ingredients with the caster sugar. Stir to combine. Whisk the eggs and milk together, stir into the bowl to mix well; beat lightly. Turn the mixture into the prepared tin and level the surface. Bake in the oven at 180°C (350°F) mark 4, for about 1½ hours until well risen and golden brown. Leave in the tin for 15 minutes before turning on to a wire rack to cool.

Chocolate sandwich

COLOUR PLATE PAGE 64

175 g (6 oz) butter or block margarine
175 g (6 oz) caster sugar
3 eggs, beaten
45 ml (2 level tbsp) cocoa powder
175 g (6 oz) self-raising flour

For the coffee butter icing
125 g (4 oz) butter
225 g (8 oz) icing sugar, sifted
90 ml (6 tbsp) coffee essence
½ quantity of Rich chocolate glacé icing (*page 72*)

Grease and base line two 19.5-cm (7½-in) sandwich tins. Cream the fat and sugar until light and fluffy and gradually beat in the egg. Mix the cocoa to a smooth paste with a little cold water and beat lightly into the creamed ingredients with the flour. Turn into the prepared tins. Bake in the oven at 180°C (350°F) mark 4 for about 30 minutes or until firm to the touch. Turn out and cool on a wire rack. Make the coffee butter icing by creaming all the ingredients together with about a third of the icing. Ice top of cake with Rich chocolate glacé icing. Use remaining butter icing to coat sides and pipe round edge of cake.

Fillings and icings

Crème au beurre

75 g (3 oz) caster sugar
60 ml (4 tbsp) water
2 egg yolks, beaten
100–175 g (4–6 oz) butter preferably unsalted

Place the sugar in a heavy-based saucepan; add the water and leave over a very low heat to dissolve the sugar, without boiling. When completely dissolved, bring to boiling point and boil steadily for 2–3 minutes, to 107°C (225°F). Pour the syrup in a thin stream on to the egg yolks in a deep bowl, whisking all the time. Continue to mix until the mixture is thick and cold. Gradually add to the creamed butter, beating well. Flavour as desired.

Variations

Chocolate Put 50 g (2 oz) chocolate dots (cooking chocolate) in a small bowl with 15 ml (1 tbsp) water. Leave to stand over hot water until the mixture is smooth and the chocolate melted. Cool slightly and beat into the basic creme au beurre.

Coffee Beat in 15–30 ml (1–2 tbsp) coffee essence to taste.

Fruit Crush 225 g (8 oz) fresh strawberries, raspberries, etc, or thaw, drain and crush frozen fruit. Beat into the basic mixture.

Orange or lemon Add freshly grated rind and juice to taste, after making the basic mixture.

Butter cream

This amount will coat the sides of an 18-cm (7-in) cake, or give a topping and a filling.

75 g (3 oz) butter
175 g (6 oz) icing sugar, sifted
vanilla essence (or other flavouring)
15–30 ml (1–2 tbsp) milk

Cream the butter until soft and gradually beat in the icing sugar, adding a few drops of vanilla essence and the milk. If you wish both to coat the sides and give a topping or filling, increase the amounts of butter and sugar to 100 g (4 oz) and 200 g (8 oz) respectively.

Variations

Orange or lemon butter cream Omit the vanilla essence and add a little finely grated orange or lemon rind and a little of the juice, beating well to avoid curdling the mixture.

Walnut butter cream Add 30 ml (2 level tbsp) finely chopped walnuts and mix well.

Almond butter cream Add 30 ml (2 level tbsp) very finely chopped toasted almonds and mix well.

Coffee butter cream Omit the vanilla essence and flavour with 10 ml (2 level tsp) instant coffee powder blended into some of the liquid, or 15 ml (1 tbsp) coffee essence.

Chocolate butter cream Flavour either by adding 25–40 g (1–1½ oz) chocolate, melted, or by adding 15 ml (1 level tbsp) cocoa blended with a little hot water (this should be cooled before it is added to the mixture).

Mocha butter cream Blend 5 ml (1 level tsp) cocoa and 10 ml (2 level tsp) instant coffee powder with a little warm water taken from the measured liquid; cool before adding to the mixture. Omit vanilla essence.

Ginger Omit vanilla essence; add 50 g (2 oz) finely chopped stem ginger.

Liqueur Omit milk and vanilla essence, add 15 ml (1 tbsp) liqueur.

Honey Omit vanilla essence and milk; add 15 ml (1 tbsp) thin honey and 15 ml (1 tbsp) lemon juice.

Fudge filling

This makes enough to sandwich three 20.5 cm (8 in) cakes together.

40 g (1½ oz) butter
450 g (1 lb) granulated sugar
150 ml (¼ pint) single cream
10 ml (2 tsp) vanilla essence

Put the butter, sugar and cream into a strong pan and heat gently, stirring, until the sugar dissolves, then boil, stirring occasionally, until a temperature of 112°C (234°F) is reached. Remove from the heat, add the essence and beat until the mixture starts to thicken, then use to sandwich layers of cake together, or use as a swirled frosting on top.

Variation

Chocolate fudge filling Add 50 g (2 oz) sweetened

chocolate, putting it into the saucepan with the butter, sugar and cream.

Fudge topping

This amount will cover an 18 cm (7 in) cake.

225 g (8 oz) icing sugar
30 ml (2 level tbsp) cocoa powder
75 g (3 oz) whipped up white vegetable fat
45 ml (3 tbsp) milk
75 g (3 oz) sugar

Sift the icing sugar and cocoa into a bowl. Heat the rest of the ingredients gently in a small pan until the sugar is dissolved. Bring to the boil, pour into the icing sugar, stir until mixed, then beat until fluffy. Spread over the cake, using a knife, rough up the surface and leave to set.

Glacé icing

This amount will cover the top of an 18 cm (7 in) cake, or up to eighteen small cakes. A quick and effective way to finish a cake is to feather ice it (see picture opposite).

100–175 g (4–6 oz) icing sugar
vanilla essence, optional
15–30 ml (1–2 tbsp) warm water

Sift the icing sugar into a basin and add a few drops of vanilla essence if used. Gradually stir in the warm water until the icing is thick enough to coat the back of a spoon. If necessary, add more water or sugar to adjust the consistency. Add a few drops of colouring if required and use at once. For icing of a finer texture, put the sugar, water and flavouring into a small pan and heat, stirring, until the mixture is warm – don't make it too hot. The icing should coat the back of a wooden spoon and look smooth and glossy.

Variations

Orange icing Substitute 15–30 ml (1–2 tbsp) strained orange juice for the water in the above recipe.

Lemon icing Substitute 15 ml (1 tbsp) strained lemon juice for the same amount of water.

Chocolate icing Blend 10 ml (2 level tsp) cocoa with a little hot water and use to replace the same amount of plain water.

Coffee icing Flavour with either 5 ml (1 tsp) coffee essence or 10 ml (2 level tsp) instant coffee powder, blended with a little of the measured water.

Mocha icing Flavour with 5 ml (1 level tsp) cocoa and 10 ml (2 level tsp) instant coffee powder, blended with a little of the measured water.

Liqueur icing Replace 10–15 ml (2–3 tsp) of the water by liqueur as desired.

Rich chocolate glacé icing

This amount will cover the top and sides of an 18 cm (7 in) cake.

75 g (3 oz) plain chocolate (or chocolate dots)
about 75 ml (5 tbsp) water
small piece of butter
225 g (8 oz) icing sugar, sifted
vanilla essence

Cut the chocolate in small pieces and put in a pan with the water; dissolve slowly over gentle heat. Add the butter when the chocolate has cooled slightly, then beat in the icing sugar gradually, with a little essence, until the mixture is glossy. If necessary, add more tepid water or more sifted icing sugar to give the correct consistency. If the icing contains many air bubbles after it has been beaten, warm it slightly and stir very gently.

American frosting

The quantities given make enough frosting for an 18 cm (7 in) cake. To make this frosting properly, it is necessary to use a sugar-boiling thermometer. Use a rotary or hand-held electric whisk.

225 g (8 oz) sugar
60 ml (4 tbsp) water
pinch of cream of tartar
1 egg white

Gently heat the sugar in the water with the cream of tartar, stirring until dissolved. Then, without stirring, boil to 120°C (240°F). Beat the egg white stiffly. Remove the sugar syrup from the heat and immediately the bubbles subside, pour it on to the egg white in a thin stream, whisking the mixture continuously. When it thickens, shows signs of going dull round the edges and is almost cold, pour it quickly over the cake and spread evenly and at once with a palette knife.

Variations

Orange frosting Add a few drops of orange essence

HOW TO FEATHER ICE

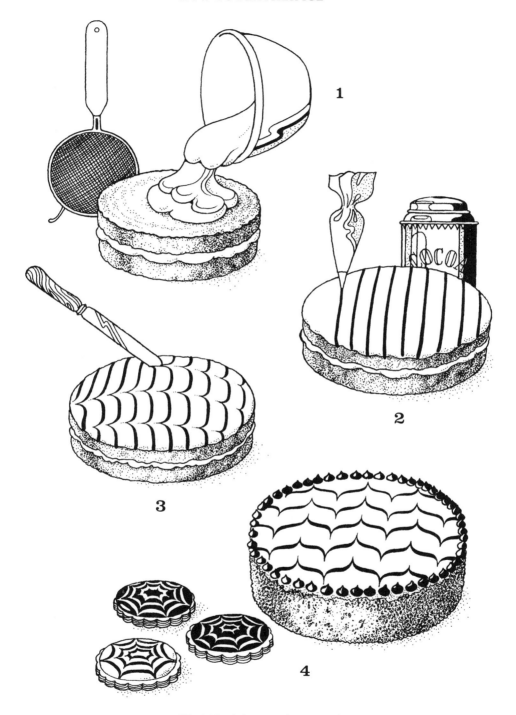

1   *Glacé icing being poured on to a cake*
2 *Using a writing nozzle in a paper piping bag containing icing of a contrasting colour,
parallel lines 2.5 cm (1 in) apart are immediately piped on*
3 *Quickly drawing a round bladed knife through the icing in alternate directions*
4 *Various feather icing designs*

SEVEN MINUTE FROSTING

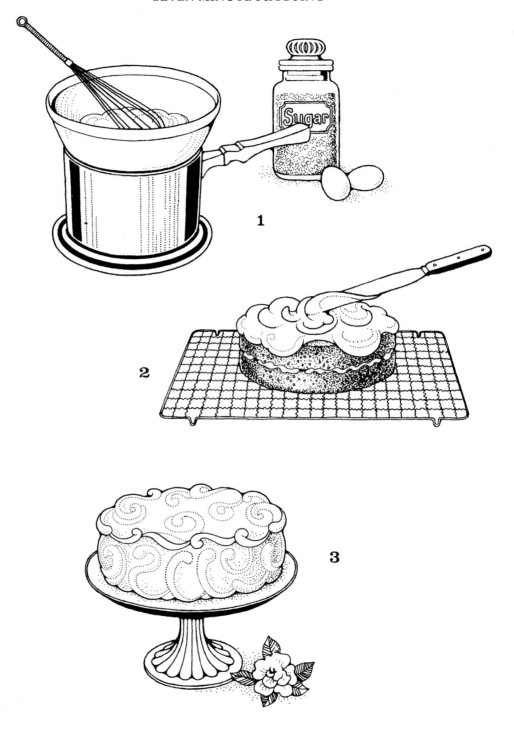

1   *Whisking all the ingredients together in a bowl over hot water*
2   *Spreading the frosting over the surface of the cake with a palette knife*
3   *Finished cake*

and a little orange colouring to the mixture while it is being beaten and before it thickens.

Lemon frosting Add a little lemon juice while beating the mixture.

Caramel frosting Substitute demerara sugar for the white sugar; follow the same method as above.

Coffee frosting Add 5 ml (1 tsp) coffee essence to the mixture while beating.

Chocolate frosting

This amount will cover an 18-cm (7-in) cake.

150 g (5 oz) icing sugar, sifted
1 egg
2.5 ml (½ tsp) vanilla essence
25 g (1 oz) plain chocolate, melted
25 g (1 oz) butter

Beat all the ingredients together in a bowl over a pan of hot water. Use immediately.

Seven minute frosting

This is an alternative to American frosting that does not set firmly and is more like marshmallow in texture. It needs no thermometer. (See picture opposite.)

1 egg white
175 g (6 oz) caster sugar
pinch of salt
30 ml (2 tbsp) water
pinch of cream of tartar

Put all the ingredients into a bowl and whisk lightly. Place the bowl over hot water and continue whisking until the mixture thickens sufficiently to hold 'peaks' – about 7 minutes, depending on the whisk used and the heat of the water. The same variations can be made as for American frosting.

Small Cakes and Cookies

Mothers of large families will find this chapter particularly useful – lots of quick recipes to keep the wolf from the door at odd moments and to fill corners of sandwich boxes for picnics. Children will find the recipes tempting. They might even like to try making some themselves – Melting moments or Flapjacks are a good choice: specially easy for beginners to make and, of course, delicious to eat. You'll find most of the ingredients in your store cupboard – a great help if you unexpectedly find yourself with time on your hands and the urge to have a baking session. If you haven't got hungry hordes descending on the day you are baking, store your cakes and cookies in separate airtight tins, or, for planning even further ahead, use the freezer. Nearly every recipe in this chapter will freeze (look at page 118 for detailed information on the subject) though many will keep well without freezing – a point worth remembering.

Some of the recipes, such as Brandy snaps and Meringues, make most useful standbys for special occasions or for serving with fruit fools and sorbets at dinner parties. These richer, more elaborate recipes are not usually quite as straightforward to make as cookies. Others, such as Macaroons, Almond crisps and Truffle cakes will make splendid Christmas presents: arrange them attractively in a special airtight container – a glass jar, for example, looks especially tempting filled with cookies and tied up with ribbon.

A tip worth remembering is how to make even-shaped cookies: shape the dough into a thick roll on a floured working surface and make sure the ends of the roll are flat. With a knife, cut the mixture – for twenty-four balls cut into six even slices, then cut each slice equally into four. This way you will get beautiful even-shaped biscuits and cookies every time.

Flapjacks

75 g (3 oz) butter or block margarine
75 g (3 oz) demerara sugar
100 g (4 oz) rolled oats

Grease a shallow 19-cm (7½-in) square tin. Cream the fat. Mix together the sugar and oats and gradually work into the creamed butter, until thoroughly blended. Press evenly into the prepared tin with a round-bladed knife. Bake in the oven at 220°C (425°F) mark 7, for about 15 minutes, until golden brown; turn the tin half-way through, to ensure even baking. Cool slightly in the tin, mark into fingers with a sharp knife and loosen round the edge; when firm, break into fingers. The flapjacks may be stored in an airtight tin for up to one week.

MAKES 12

Rich ginger flapjacks

50 g (2 oz) butter or block margarine
50 g (2 oz) demerara sugar
45 ml (3 tbsp) golden syrup
125 g (4 oz) rolled oats
2.5 ml (½ level tsp) ground ginger

Grease an 18-cm (7-in) sandwich cake tin. Melt the fat with the sugar and syrup and pour it on to the mixed rolled oats and ginger. Mix well, put the mixture into the prepared tin and press down well. Bake in the oven at 180°C (350°F) mark 4, for 20–25 minutes. Leave to cool in the tin and cut into fingers when cool.

MAKES 6–8

Gingernuts

100 g (4 oz) self-raising flour
2.5 ml (½ level tsp) bicarbonate of soda
5–10 ml (1–2 level tsp) ground ginger
5 ml (1 level tsp) ground cinnamon, optional
10 ml (2 level tsp) caster sugar
50 g (2 oz) butter or block margarine
75 g (3 oz) golden syrup

Grease two baking sheets. Sift together the flour, bicarbonate of soda, ginger, cinnamon and sugar. Melt the fat, and stir in the syrup. Stir these into the dry ingredients and mix well. Roll the dough into small balls, place well apart on the greased baking sheets and flatten slightly. Bake in the oven at 190°C (375°F) mark 5, for about 15 minutes. The gingernuts will have the traditional cracked tops. Cool for a few minutes before lifting carefully from the baking sheet.

Finish cooling on a wire rack and then store in an airtight tin.

If liked, these biscuits may be iced with lemon-flavoured glacé icing (see page 72).

MAKES ABOUT 24

Grantham gingerbreads

COLOUR PLATE PAGE 65

250 g (9 oz) self-raising flour
5 ml (1 level tsp) ground ginger
100 g (4 oz) butter or block margarine
350 g (12 oz) caster sugar
1 egg, beaten

Grease two to three baking sheets. Sift the flour and ginger together. Cream the fat and sugar and beat in the egg gradually. Stir in the flour and ginger until a fairly firm dough is obtained. Roll into small balls about the size of a walnut and put them on the baking sheets. Bake in the oven at 150°C (300°F) mark 2, for 40–45 minutes, until they are crisp, hollow and very lightly browned.

MAKES 30

Custard creams

75 g (3 oz) block margarine
75 g (3 oz) caster sugar
1 egg, beaten
50 g (1½ oz) custard powder
150 g (5½ oz) self-raising flour
30 ml (2 tbsp) red jam

For the icing
100 g (4 oz) icing sugar
water

Grease three baking sheets. Cream margarine and caster sugar well together until light and fluffy, then beat in the egg. Sieve together custard powder and flour, and stir this in too. Knead lightly, then roll out mixture on a lightly floured surface. Use a small fluted round cutter to stamp out thirty biscuits. Warm the jam. Cool slightly, then brush fifteen of the biscuits with the jam. Sandwich biscuits in pairs together with the jam in the middle. Place on greased baking sheets and bake in oven at 170°C (325°F) mark 3 for about 15 minutes. Cool on a wire rack.

Make up a thick glacé icing using the icing sugar and a little water. Using a piping bag fitted with a small plain nozzle, pipe zigzag lines on top of the biscuits or place a blob on each biscuit.

MAKES 15

Boston brownies

75 g (2½ oz) butter or block margarine
50 g (2 oz) plain chocolate
175 g (6 oz) caster sugar
75 g (2½ oz) self-raising flour
1.25 ml (¼ level tsp) salt
2 eggs, beaten
2.5 ml (½ tsp) vanilla essence
50 g (2 oz) walnuts, roughly chopped

Grease and flour a shallow 20.5-cm (8-in) square tin. Melt the fat and chocolate in a basin over hot water and add the sugar. Sift the flour with the salt and add the chocolate mixture, eggs, vanilla essence and walnuts. Beat until smooth and pour into the tin. Bake in the oven at 180°C (350°F) mark 4, for 35–40 minutes, until the mixture is risen and begins to leave the sides of the tin. Leave in the tin to cool, then cut into fingers.

MAKES 12

Date chews

1 large egg
25 g (1 oz) caster sugar
1.25 ml (¼ level tsp) salt
15 g (½ oz) butter, melted
225 g (8 oz) stoned dates, chopped
25 g (1 oz) shelled walnuts, chopped
75 g (3 oz) self-raising flour
10 ml (2 tsp) hot water
caster sugar to dredge

Grease and line a shallow tin measuring 15 × 23 cm (6 × 9 in). In a bowl beat together the egg, sugar, salt and butter. Stir in the dates and nuts. Beat in the flour alternately with the water. Spread the mixture over the lined tin and bake in the oven at 180°C (350°F) mark 4, for about 30 minutes. Dredge with caster sugar and cool on a wire rack. Cut into squares.

MAKES ABOUT 12

Macaroons

COLOUR PLATE PAGE 65

1 egg white
50 g (2 oz) ground almonds
100 g (3½ oz) caster sugar
2.5 ml (½ tsp) almond essence
few split almonds
little egg white to glaze

Line one or two baking sheets with non-stick paper or rice paper. Whisk the egg white until stiff and fold in the ground almonds, caster sugar and almond essence. Place spoonfuls of the mixture on the non-stick paper, leaving plenty of room for spreading. (Alternatively, pipe the mixture on to the paper, using a piping bag and 1-cm (½-in) plain nozzle.) Top each biscuit with a split almond and brush with egg white. Bake in the oven at 180°C (350°F) mark 4, for 20–25 minutes, until just beginning to colour. Cool on a wire rack.

MAKES 10

Swiss tartlets

COLOUR PLATE PAGE 65

100 g (4 oz) butter
25 g (1 oz) caster sugar
vanilla essence
100 g (4 oz) plain flour
icing sugar
redcurrant jelly

Arrange six greaseproof paper baking cases in small patty tins. Cream the butter and sugar very thoroughly, until light and fluffy. Beat in a few drops of vanilla essence. Gradually add the flour, beating very well after each addition. Place the mixture in a piping bag fitted with a large star vegetable nozzle. Pipe it into the paper cases, starting at the centre, piping with a spiral motion round the sides, leaving a shallow depression in the centre. Bake in the oven at 180°C (350°F) mark 4, for 20–25 minutes. Cool on a wire rack. When cold, dredge with icing sugar and place a little redcurrant jelly in the centre.

MAKES 6

Coconut castles

100 g (4 oz) butter or block margarine
100 g (4 oz) caster sugar
2 eggs, beaten
100 g (4 oz) self-raising flour
red jam, sieved
desiccated coconut
glacé cherries and angelica

Grease 10–12 dariole moulds. Cream the fat and sugar until pale and fluffy. Add the egg a little at a time, beating well after each addition. Fold in half the flour, using a tablespoon, then fold in the rest. Three-quarters fill the moulds and bake in the oven at 180°C (350°F) mark 4, for about 20 minutes, or until firm and browned. Turn them out of the moulds to cool on a wire rack. Trim off the bottoms, so that the cakes stand firmly and are of even height. When they are nearly cold, brush with melted jam, holding them on a skewer, then roll them in coconut. Top each 'castle' with a glacé cherry and two angelica 'leaves'.

MAKES 10–12

Almond crisps

COLOUR PLATE PAGE 65

125 g (4 oz) butter
75 g (3 oz) caster sugar
1 egg yolk
few drops of almond essence
150 g (5 oz) self-raising flour
75 g (3 oz) nibbed almonds

Cream together the butter and sugar until light and fluffy. Beat in the egg yolk and almond essence and finally the flour, to give a smooth dough. Form into a neat log shape and cut into twenty-four even slices. Shape each into a ball, then roll in nibbed almonds. Place well apart on greased baking sheets and bake at 190°C (375°F) mark 5, for 15–20 minutes. Cool on a wire rack.

MAKES ABOUT 24

Walnut crisps

These are made as Almond crisps (see above) with the following differences:

Omit almond essence and nibbed almonds. Sift 5 ml (1 level tsp) ground cinnamon with the flour. Roll mixture lightly into balls and place, well apart, on greased baking sheets. Press half a shelled walnut on alternate cookies. Bake as above. When cold, sandwich in pairs with cinnamon-flavoured butter cream.

Fluted caraway buns

75 g (3 oz) butter or block margarine
50 g (2 oz) caster sugar
2 eggs
30 ml (2 level tbsp) lemon curd
125 g (4 oz) self-raising flour
pinch of salt
2.5 ml ($\frac{1}{2}$ level tsp) caraway seeds
glacé icing, optional
glacé cherries, optional

Grease nine fluted patty tins about 7 cm ($2\frac{3}{4}$ in) wide and 3 cm ($1\frac{1}{4}$ in) deep. Cream together the fat and

caster sugar and beat in the eggs. Alternatively fold in the lemon curd and flour sifted with the salt. Lastly fold in the caraway seeds. Divide between the patty tins and bake in the oven at 170°C (325°F) mark 3, for about 25 minutes. Turn out and cool on a wire rack bottom sides up. Decorate each with a little knob of stiff glacé icing and half a glacé cherry; or serve the other way up, simply dusted with icing sugar.

MAKES 9

Melting moments

100 g (4 oz) butter or block margarine
75 g (3 oz) sugar
1 egg yolk
few drops of vanilla essence
150 g (5 oz) self-raising flour
crushed cornflakes

Grease two baking sheets. Cream the fat and sugar together and beat in the egg yolk. Flavour with vanilla essence, stir in the flour to give a stiff dough and divide the mixture into twenty to twenty-four portions. Form each piece into a ball and roll in crushed cornflakes. Place the balls on the baking sheets well apart and bake in the oven at 190°C (375°F) mark 5, for 15–20 minutes. Cool on the baking sheets for a few moments before lifting on to a wire rack.

MAKES 20–24

Honey coffee crunchies

100 g (4 oz) hazel nuts
100 g (4 oz) butter
65 g ($2\frac{1}{2}$ oz) caster sugar
150 g (5 oz) plain flour
30 ml (2 level tbsp) thick honey

For the coffee glacé icing
100 g (4 oz) icing sugar
10 ml (2 tsp) coffee essence
15 ml (3 tsp) water

Grease two baking sheets. Place the nuts in a tin in the oven until the skins loosen; remove the skins by rubbing the nuts in a paper bag. Reserve thirty-six nuts and grind the remainder finely, about half at a time, in an electric or hand operated grinder. Cream the butter and sugar until light and creamy. Gradually stir in the ground nuts and flour. Leave the dough in a cool place until of a rolling consistency. Roll out on a floured surface to about 0.3 cm ($\frac{1}{8}$ in) thickness. Cut out rounds, using a 6.5-cm ($2\frac{1}{2}$-in) plain cutter. Lift carefully on to the greased baking sheets and bake in the oven at 180°C (350°F) mark 4, for 10–15 minutes, until lightly coloured. Cool, then sandwich in pairs with honey. Ice the centres with coffee icing, top with three whole hazel nuts and leave until set.

MAKES 12 PAIRS

Brandy snaps

50 g (2 oz) butter or block margarine
50 g (2 oz) caster sugar
50 g (2 oz) golden syrup – about 30 ml (2 tbsp)
50 g (2 oz) plain flour
2.5 ml (½ level tsp) ground ginger
5 ml (1 tsp) brandy (optional)
grated rind of ½ lemon
whipped cream

Grease the handles of several wooden spoons and line two or three baking sheets with non-stick paper. Melt the fat with the sugar and syrup in a small saucepan over a low heat. Remove from the heat and stir in the sifted flour and ginger, brandy and lemon rind. Drop small spoonfuls of the mixture about 10 cm (4 in)

apart on the lined baking sheets, to allow plenty of room for spreading. Bake in rotation in the oven at 180°C (350°F) mark 4, for 7–10 minutes, until bubbly and golden. Allow to cool for 1–2 minutes, then loosen with a palette knife and roll them round the spoon handles. Leave until set, then twist gently to remove. (If the biscuits cool too much whilst still on the sheet and become too brittle to roll, return the sheet to the oven for a moment to soften them.) Fill the brandy snaps with whipped cream just before serving. Brandy snaps can be stored unfilled for about a week in an airtight tin.

MAKES 10

Peanut butter cookies

50 g (2 oz) peanut butter
grated rind of ½ orange
50 g (2 oz) caster sugar
45 ml (3 level tbsp) light, soft brown sugar
50 g (2 oz) butter
1 standard egg or ½ large egg
30 ml (2 level tbsp) raisins, stoned and chopped
100 g (4 oz) self-raising flour

BRANDY SNAPS

1   Rolling the brandy snaps round the handle of a wooden spoon
2   Finished brandy snaps

Mille-feuilles

Cream together the peanut butter, orange rind, sugars and butter until light and fluffy. Beat in the egg, add the raisins and stir in the flour to make a fairly firm dough. Roll the dough into small balls about the size of a walnut and place well apart on an ungreased baking sheet; dip a fork in a little flour and press criss-cross lines on each ball. Bake in the oven at 180°C (350°F) mark 4, for about 25 minutes, until risen and golden brown. Cool on a wire rack.

MAKES 25–30

spoon or spatula and finish with the finger tips. Knead lightly to form a ball. Roll out carefully on a lightly floured surface to about 0.3 cm ($\frac{1}{8}$ in) thick – the mixture will be crumbly and will need moulding together between rollings. Stamp out rounds using a 6.5-cm (2$\frac{1}{2}$-in) fluted cutter or cut into fingers. Bake in the centre of the oven or just below at 150°C (300°F) mark 2, for about 25 minutes until lightly tinged with colour. Cool on a wire rack. To serve, dredge with caster sugar.

MAKES ABOUT 9

Truffle cakes

100 g (4 oz) plain cake or cake trimmings
100 g (4 oz) caster sugar
100 g (4 oz) ground almonds
apricot jam, sieved
sherry or rum to flavour
chocolate vermicelli

Rub the cake through a fairly coarse sieve and add the caster sugar, ground almonds and enough apricot jam to bind. Flavour as liked with sherry or rum. Shape the mixture into small balls and leave to become firm. Dip each ball into the jam and roll in chocolate vermicelli. When dry, put into small paper cases.

MAKES 16–18

Chocolate crackles

225 g (8 oz) chocolate dots
15 ml (1 tbsp) golden syrup
50 g (2 oz) butter or block margarine
50 g (2 oz) cornflakes or Rice Crispies

Place twelve paper cases on a baking sheet. Melt the chocolate dots with the golden syrup and fat over a low heat, or put in a basin set over a pan of hot water. Fold in the cornflakes or Crispies. When well mixed, divide between the paper cases and leave to set.

MAKES 12

One-two-three biscuits

50 g (2 oz) butter
25 g (1 oz) caster sugar
75 g (3 oz) plain flour
caster sugar to dredge

Grease one or two baking sheets. Cream the butter and sugar well together. Work in the flour using a

Oatmeal cookies

175 g (6 oz) plain flour
100 g (4 oz) caster sugar
2.5 ml ($\frac{1}{2}$ level tsp) baking powder
1.25 ml ($\frac{1}{4}$ level tsp) bicarbonate of soda
2.5 ml ($\frac{1}{2}$ level tsp) salt
2.5 ml ($\frac{1}{2}$ level tsp) ground cinnamon
150 g (5 oz) rolled oats
75 g (3 oz) raisins
150 ml ($\frac{1}{4}$ pint) vegetable oil
1 egg
60 ml (4 tbsp) milk

Sift together the dry ingredients. Add rolled oats and raisins and beat in the oil, egg and milk. When stiff enough to need pushing off the spoon, put in teaspoonfuls on ungreased baking sheets about 4 cm (1$\frac{1}{2}$ in) apart. Bake in the oven at 200°C (400°F) mark 6, for 10–12 minutes. Cool on a wire rack.

MAKES 36

Uncooked chocolate cake

100 g (4 oz) sweet biscuits
50 g (2 oz) digestive biscuits
50 g (2 oz) shelled walnuts or seedless raisins
100 g (3$\frac{1}{2}$ oz) butter or block margarine
25 g (1 oz) caster sugar
75 g (3 oz) golden syrup
50 g (2 oz) cocoa

For the icing
50 g (2 oz) cooking chocolate
15 ml (1 tbsp) hot water
65 g (2$\frac{1}{2}$ oz) icing sugar
knob of butter

Put a 19- or 20.5-cm (7$\frac{1}{2}$- or 8-in) flan ring on a flat serving plate. Roughly crush the biscuits with a rolling pin. Coarsely chop the walnuts or raisins and

Christmas cake

mix with the biscuits. Cream together the fat, sugar and syrup. Beat in the sifted cocoa and work in the biscuits and walnuts or raisins. When the ingredients are well mixed, press evenly into the flan ring and leave overnight in a cold place – preferably the refrigerator. The next day remove the flan ring, spread the icing over the top of the cake and leave to set.

To make the icing put the chocolate, hot water, sifted icing sugar and butter in a small saucepan and stir together over a very low heat until the chocolate has melted. Use when of a coating consistency.

Chocolate date bars

These are best eaten the day after making, but can be kept up to 1 week – preferably in one piece.

100 g (4 oz) self-raising flour
150 g (5 oz) rolled oats
100 g (4 oz) light soft brown sugar
175 g (6 oz) butter, melted

For the filling
175 g (6 oz) stoned dates, chopped
10 ml (2 level tsp) flour
150 ml ($\frac{1}{4}$ pint) water
100 g (4 oz) chocolate dots
vanilla essence

Grease and line the base of an oblong tin measuring 30.5 × 10 × 2.5 cm (12 × 14 × 1 in). To make the filling put the dates, flour, water, chocolate and a few drops of essence in a small saucepan and cook gently for 10 minutes. Leave to cool while preparing the crumble mixture.

In a bowl mix together the flour, oats and sugar and stir in the butter. Spread half the crumble over the base of the prepared tin, pressing well down. Cover with filling, then the remainder of the crumble. Press down with a round-bladed knife. Bake in centre of the oven at 190°C (375°F) mark 5, for about 25 minutes, until golden brown. Cool in the tin for 15 minutes, then turn out on to a board or other flat surface. To serve, cut into fingers.
MAKES 12

Meringues

2 egg whites
40–50 g (1$\frac{1}{2}$–2 oz) granulated sugar
40–50 g (1$\frac{1}{2}$–2 oz) caster sugar
142 ml ($\frac{1}{4}$ pint) whipping or double cream

Line a baking sheet with a sheet of kitchen foil and rub a trace of vegetable oil over the surface or line it with non-stick paper. Whisk the egg whites very stiffly, add the granulated sugar and whisk again until the mixture regains its former stiffness. Lastly, fold in the caster sugar very lightly, using a metal spoon. Pipe through a forcing bag (*see page 109*) or put in spoonfuls on to the baking sheet and dry off in the oven for several hours at 130°C (250°F) mark $\frac{1}{2}$, until the meringues are firm and crisp but still white; if they begin to brown, prop the oven door open a little. When they are cool, sandwich them together with whipped cream.
MAKES 12–16 MERINGUE SHELLS

Variations
1 To make pink meringues, add 1–2 drops of red colouring to the sugar.
2 To make coffee meringues, use coffee essence, adding 5 ml (1 tsp) to each egg white when the sugar is folded in.
3 For chocolate meringues, add cocoa with the caster sugar, allowing 5 ml (1 level tsp) cocoa for each egg white.
4 Add finely chopped nuts, melted chocolate or a liqueur to the filling.

Chocolate frosties

100 g (4 oz) whole unblanched almonds
200 g (7 oz) self-raising flour
150 g (5 oz) caster sugar
1.25 ml ($\frac{1}{4}$ level tsp) ground nutmeg
150 g (5 oz) butter or block margarine
50 g (2 oz) plain chocolate, coarsely grated
1 egg, beaten

Grease three baking sheets. Grind almonds without blanching until they resemble fine crumbs. Sift flour, sugar and nutmeg into a bowl. Rub fat into flour mixture until it resembles fine breadcrumbs. Stir in the ground almonds and 25 g (1 oz) grated chocolate. Bind together with egg until smooth. Divide mixture into two and roll each part into a 30.5-cm (12-in) long thin sausage shape, using greaseproof or non-stick paper. Chill in the ice cube compartment of the refrigerator until firm – about 30 minutes. Cut slices off at an angle, about 1 cm ($\frac{1}{2}$ in) thick. Place well apart on the greased baking sheets. Bake in the oven at 190°C (375°F) mark 5, for 15–20 minutes. Cool until just warm then sprinkle remaining grated chocolate over. Transfer to wire rack.
MAKES ABOUT 48

Vanilla frosties

Omit nutmeg, whole egg and chocolate. Use 15 ml (1 tbsp) beaten egg and 7.5 ml (1½ tsp) vanilla essence. Shape into rolls about 7.5 cm (3 in) long and 1 cm (½ in) in diameter. Form into crescents on greased baking sheets. Bake as above.

MAKES ABOUT 36

Florentines

COLOUR PLATE PAGE 65

100 g (3½ oz) butter
100 g (4 oz) caster sugar
100 g (4 oz) chopped nuts (walnuts and almonds mixed if possible)
30 ml (2 level tbsp) chopped sultanas
5 glacé cherries, chopped
30 ml (2 level tbsp) finely chopped mixed peel
15 ml (1 tbsp) cream or top of the milk
100 g (4 oz) plain chocolate

Line two or three baking sheets with non-stick paper. Melt the butter, add the sugar and boil together for 1 minute. Stir in all the other ingredients except the chocolate and mix well. Drop the mixture in small, well-rounded heaps on to the baking sheets, keeping them far apart to allow for spreading – allow four per sheet. Bake in the oven at 180°C (350°F) mark 4, for about 10 minutes, until golden brown. When you take the biscuits out of the oven, press the edges to a neat shape with a knife. When they are beginning to go firm, remove the biscuits carefully and cool on a wire rack. To finish, spread the backs of the biscuits with melted chocolate and mark lines across with a fork. Store in an airtight tin, separated by non-stick paper.

MAKES ABOUT 12

Walnut nuggets

125 g (4½ oz) block margarine
125 g (4½ oz) caster sugar
1 egg, beaten
grated rind of 1 orange
225 g (8 oz) plain flour
1.25 ml (¼ level tsp) ground cinnamon
50 g (2 oz) shelled walnuts, chopped

FLORENTINES

1   *Spreading with melted chocolate*
2   *Using fork to make criss-cross lines*

Grease two baking sheets. Cream margarine and sugar together until light and fluffy. Beat in egg and orange rind. Fold in the flour, cinnamon and walnuts. Place in teaspoonfuls on the greased baking sheets, and bake in oven at 180°C (350°F) mark 4, for about 15 minutes. Cool on a wire rack.

MAKES 18

Coffee kisses

175 g (6 oz) butter
75 g (3 oz) caster sugar
30 ml (2 tbsp) beaten egg
20 ml (4 tsp) coffee essence
150 g (5 oz) plain flour
175 g (6 oz) icing sugar

Grease three baking sheets. Soften 75 g (3 oz) of the butter and cream with the caster sugar until pale and smooth. Gradually spoon in the beaten egg and 15 ml (3 tsp) coffee essence. Stir in the sifted flour. Spoon into a forcing bag fitted with a medium star vegetable nozzle. Pipe about thirty small whirls on to the greased baking sheets. The rosettes will spread slightly so pipe fairly well apart. Bake in the oven at 200°C (400°F) mark 6, for about 12 minutes until pale golden. Cool on a wire rack.

For the filling, cream together the remaining 100 g (3 oz) butter and the icing sugar, beat in 5 ml (1 tsp) coffee essence. Pair rosettes together with a whirl of the coffee cream inside.

MAKES 15

Lemon sugar cookies

No rolling is needed for this recipe. Just criss-cross with a fork before baking.

225 g (8 oz) plain flour
about 5 ml (¾ level tsp) baking powder
pinch of salt
pinch of ground nutmeg
100 ml (4 fl oz) vegetable oil
100 g (4 oz) caster sugar
1 egg
grated rind of 1 small lemon
granulated sugar

Lightly grease some baking sheets. Sift together the dry ingredients. Combine oil and sugar in a basin, beat in egg and lemon rind. Add dry ingredients to the oil mixture, blend well and shape into balls about 2 cm (¾ in) in diameter. Dip tops of balls into granulated sugar and place, sugar side up, on the greased baking sheets about 5 cm (2 in) apart. Criss-cross the biscuits with the prongs of a fork, impressing a pattern. Bake in oven at 190°C (375°F) mark 5, for 10–12 minutes. Cool on a wire rack.

MAKES 30

Hazel nut bars

100 g (4 oz) hazel nuts
225 g (8 oz) plain flour
175 g (6 oz) butter
100 g (4 oz) icing sugar
1 egg white
7.5 ml (½ tbsp) coffee essence

Place hazel nuts in a tin and roast until beginning to brown in a moderately hot oven. Place in a paper bag and rub to remove skin. Chop the nuts. Sift the flour into a mound on a working surface. Make a well in the centre, add the butter cut in small pieces, and the icing sugar. Work butter and icing sugar together using fingertips. When pale and creamy, gradually work in the flour, using the fingertips. Knead in the hazel nuts and work to a smooth dough. Divide the dough into two parts. Roll out lightly on a floured surface to about 0.3–0.5 cm (⅛–¼ in) thickness. The dough needs careful handling. With a knife mark down lightly in a criss-cross pattern. Brush over with a little lightly whisked egg white and coffee essence mixed together. Cut into fingers about 7.5 × 4 cm (3 × 1½ in). Lift carefully on to ungreased baking sheets. Bake at 180°C (350°F) mark 4, for about 15 minutes until lightly coloured. Cool on a wire rack.

MAKES ABOUT 32

Walnut crunchies

These are at their best freshly baked. Keep a roll of the dough in the refrigerator for up to three days to slice off and bake when the oven is on anyway.

75 g (3 oz) butter
150 g (5 oz) demerara sugar
1 large egg
15 ml (1 tbsp) coffee essence
75 g (3 oz) walnuts, finely chopped
175 g (6 oz) self-raising flour

Lightly grease about three or four baking sheets. Cream butter, beat in sugar until thoroughly creamed, then beat in egg. Stir in coffee essence, walnuts and flour. When well blended, shape into a

23-cm (9-in) long roll on a lightly floured surface. Wrap in foil or greaseproof paper. Chill in the refrigerator until required – up to three days. To cook, remove from the refrigerator, slice thinly, place slices well apart on greased baking sheets, bake in the oven at 200°C (400°F) mark 6, for about 10 minutes. Cool on a wire rack.

MAKES ABOUT 36

Caramel shortbread

175 g (6 oz) plain flour
50 g (2 oz) caster sugar
175 g (6 oz) butter
50 g (2 oz) soft brown sugar
1 large can condensed milk
100 g (4 oz) plain chocolate

Sift flour into a basin, add caster sugar and rub in 125 g (4 oz) butter lightly with fingertips until the mixture resembles fine crumbs. Press mixture evenly into a Swiss roll tin measuring 29 × 19 cm (11½ × 7½ in). Bake at 170°C (325°F) mark 3, for about 30 minutes until just coloured. Allow to cool.

Heat the remaining butter and the soft brown sugar together in a saucepan. Stir in the condensed milk and heat gently until the sugar dissolves. Bring to the boil and stir continuously until the caramel mixture is a creamy fudge colour. Pour over the shortbread and spread evenly. Leave to cool. Melt the chocolate in a basin over hot but not boiling water and pour over the caramel. Tap tin on a hard surface to level the chocolate. Leave to set then cut in fingers.

Coconut and orange bars

150 g (5 oz) butter
100 g (4 oz) caster sugar
2 eggs, beaten
grated rind of 1 orange
orange juice
100 g (3½ oz) self-raising flour
50 g (2 oz) desiccated coconut
50 g (2 oz) long thread coconut

For the icing
100 g (4 oz) icing sugar
yellow food colouring

Grease and line a cake tin with 28 × 18 cm (11 × 7 in) top measurements. Cream the butter, add sugar and continue creaming until light and fluffy. Beat in eggs

a little at a time. Stir in orange rind and 30 ml (2 tbsp) of the juice. Lightly beat in the sifted flour and desiccated coconut. Spread creamed mixture into the prepared tin. Sprinkle long thread coconut over the mixture and press lightly into it. Bake in the oven at 180°C (350°F) mark 4, for about 25 minutes until firm. Turn out and cool on a wire rack.

To make the icing, sift icing sugar into a basin and mix enough orange juice to give a coating consistency. Add a drop or two of colouring. Drizzle icing over cake with a teaspoon. Leave to set then cut into bars.

Orange chip cookies

100 g (4 oz) butter or block margarine
75 g (3 oz) caster sugar
½ large egg, beaten
grated rind of 1 orange
50 g (2 oz) chocolate dots
100 g (4 oz) self-raising flour

Cream together the fat and sugar until light and fluffy. Beat in the egg, then stir in the orange rind, chocolate and flour to make a soft dough. Roll dough into twenty-four to thirty balls about the size of a shelled walnut and place well apart on an ungreased baking sheet. Make a criss-cross pattern on top of each with a fork pressed into each ball. Bake in the oven at 180°C (350°F) mark 4, for about 25 minutes. Cool on a wire rack.

MAKES 24–30

Spiced blackcurrant bars

225 g (8 oz) plain flour
10 ml (2 level tsp) baking powder
10 ml (2 level tsp) ground mixed spice
5 ml (1 level tsp) ground cinnamon
100 g (4 oz) butter
150 g (5 oz) caster sugar
15 ml (1 level tbsp) golden syrup
1 large egg
225 g (8 oz) blackcurrant jam
75 g (3 oz) shelled walnuts, coarsely chopped

Grease and line two shallow cake tins with 30.5 × 10 cm (12 × 4 in) top measurements. Sift together the flour, baking powder and spices. Cream butter and sugar until pale in colour. Add the syrup and egg, beat well. Fold the dry ingredients into the creamed mixture. Wrap loosely and chill in the refrigerator until firm – about 1 hour. Coarsely grate half the chilled dough into the base of the tins. Press down lightly and spread the well-stirred blackcurrant jam over them. Grate the remaining dough on to the jam. Top with nuts. Bake in the oven at 180°C (350°F) mark 4, for about 30 minutes. Leave to cool in the tins. When cold, cut into bars.

MAKES ABOUT 24

Date squares

225 g (8 oz) stoned dates, chopped
30 ml (2 tbsp) lemon juice
30 ml (2 tbsp) water
175 g (6 oz) butter
175 g (6 oz) demerara sugar
225 g (8 oz) rolled oats
pinch of salt

Grease a 19-cm ($7\frac{1}{2}$-in) shallow square tin. Place chopped dates, lemon juice and water in a saucepan and heat gently until softened and well blended. Heat butter and sugar in another saucepan until the butter melts. Take butter mixture off the heat and stir in the rolled oats and salt. Press half the oat mixture into the base of the greased tin. Spread the date mixture over it then finish with another layer of oats. Press down well. Bake at 180°C (350°F) mark 4, for 50–55 minutes until golden brown and firm. When cold, remove from tin and cut into squares.

MAKES 16

Ginger fridge cookies

225 g (8 oz) plain flour
2.5 ml ($\frac{1}{2}$ level tsp) bicarbonate of soda
2.5 ml ($\frac{1}{2}$ level tsp) salt
5 ml (1 level tsp) ground ginger
100 ml (4 fl oz) vegetable oil
100 g (4 oz) soft brown sugar
100 g (4 oz) caster sugar
1 egg
2.5 ml ($\frac{1}{2}$ tsp) vanilla essence
50 g (2 oz) flaked almonds

Sift together the dry ingredients. Beat oil, sugars, egg and essence together. Add to dry ingredients with the nuts. Work together to give a manageable dough. Shape into a roll and wrap in greaseproof paper. Chill in the refrigerator until needed. Cut into thin slices and bake on lightly greased baking sheets in the oven at 200°C (400°F) mark 6, for about 10 minutes. Cool on a wire rack.

MAKES ABOUT 36

Rock buns

225 g (8 oz) plain flour
pinch of salt
10 ml (2 level tsp) baking powder
50 g (2 oz) butter
50 g (2 oz) lard
75 g (3 oz) demerara sugar
75 g (3 oz) mixed dried fruit
grated rind of $\frac{1}{2}$ lemon
1 egg, beaten
milk

Lightly grease two baking sheets. Sift together the flour, salt and baking powder. Rub in the butter and lard until it resembles fine breadcrumbs. Add the sugar, fruit and lemon rind. Mix thoroughly. Using a fork, mix to a moist but stiff dough with the beaten egg and a little milk. Using two forks shape into really rocky heaps on greased baking sheets. Bake at 200°C (400°F) mark 6, for about 20 minutes until golden brown. Cool on a wire rack and serve fresh.

MAKES 12

Chocolate bourbons

100 g (4 oz) plain flour
25 g (1 oz) cornflour
25 g (1 oz) drinking chocolate powder
75 g (3 oz) butter
75 g (3 oz) caster sugar
milk to mix, if required

For the filling
50 g (2 oz) butter
75 g (3 oz) icing sugar
15 ml (1 level tbsp) drinking chocolate
  powder

Grease two to three baking sheets. Sift together the flour, cornflour and drinking chocolate. Cream the butter and caster sugar until light and fluffy, then gradually work in the sifted ingredients with a little milk if necessary to give a fairly stiff dough. (This may be a little difficult to achieve but if the dough is too soft, the texture of the finished biscuits will be tough.) Knead lightly, roll out to about 0.3-cm ($\frac{1}{8}$-in) thickness between non-stick paper and cut into 2.5 × 7.5 cm (1 × 3 in) fingers using a fluted pastry wheel. Place on the greased baking sheets and bake in the oven at 190°C (375°F) mark 5, for about 10 minutes. Cool on a wire rack.

To make the chocolate filling, cream the butter until soft, beat in the sifted icing sugar and

chocolate. Sandwich biscuits in pairs with filling.
MAKES 16

Mincemeat cinnamon meltaways

225 g (8 oz) plain flour
10 ml (2 level tsp) cream of tartar
5 ml (1 level tsp) bicarbonate of soda
2.5 ml ($\frac{1}{2}$ level tsp) ground cinnamon
pinch of salt
100 g (4 oz) butter or block margarine
100 g (4 oz) caster sugar
1 egg, beaten
225 g (8 oz) mincemeat
flaked almonds

Sift together the flour, cream of tartar, bicarbonate of soda, cinnamon and salt. Rub in the fat, add the sugar, mix to a soft dough with the egg. Knead lightly and roll out to about 0.3-cm ($\frac{1}{8}$-in) thickness on a well-floured surface or between sheets of waxed or non-stick paper: handle with care. Stamp out bases and lids with a plain cutter to line about sixteen 6.5-cm ($2\frac{1}{2}$-in) diameter (top measurement) patty pans. Place bases in the pans and add about a teaspoonful of mincemeat. Top with lid, which seals itself during cooking; scatter nuts over lids. Bake in oven at 200°C (400°F) mark 6, for about 15 minutes. Leave to cool a little, then slip out on to a wire rack to cool further.
MAKES ABOUT 16

Cup cakes

100 g (4 oz) butter
100 g (4 oz) caster sugar
2 eggs, beaten
100 g (4 oz) self-raising flour
50 g (2 oz) shelled walnuts, chopped (or raisins, cherries, chocolate dots, etc)

For the icing
350 g (12 oz) icing sugar
45 ml (3 tbsp) hot water

Place eighteen paper cases in patty tins. Cream butter and caster sugar until light and fluffy. Gradually beat in eggs, then fold in flour and nuts or fruit. Mix well. Divide mixture between paper cases and bake in the oven at 190°C (375°F) mark 5, for about 20 minutes until golden brown. Cool on a wire rack. Make up glacé icing by mixing sifted icing sugar with water. When the cakes are cold cover the top of each with a little icing.
MAKES 18

Queen cakes
Use the basic cup cake recipe above but with the addition of 50 g (2 oz) sultanas and bake in greased shell bun tins.

Raspberry buns

150 g (5 oz) self-raising flour
pinch of salt
75 g (3 oz) ground rice
75 g (3 oz) caster sugar
50 g (2 oz) butter
2 eggs, lightly beaten
raspberry jam

For the topping
a little beaten egg
coffee sugar crystals

Lightly grease two baking sheets. In a bowl mix together the flour, salt, ground rice and caster sugar. Add the butter and rub in until the mixture resembles fine breadcrumbs. Add eggs and mix well to form a stiff dough. Form into ten balls and place well apart on the baking sheets. Make a hole in the centre of each and fill with a little raspberry jam. Close up the opening and brush with beaten egg. Sprinkle with sugar crystals and bake in the oven at 220°C (425°F) mark 7, for about 15 minutes. Cool on a wire rack. Eat really fresh.
MAKES 10

Pastries and Gâteaux

In this chapter are some of the confections which make your mouth water as you pass by patisseries and coffee shops. They are perhaps most popular in Switzerland and Austria, though France and Denmark are also famous for their pastries.

The question probably uppermost in your mind is: can you *really* make these cakes and pastries at home? We can't turn you into a professional patissière over night but if you follow these recipes *to the letter* – no cheating or cutting corners – we promise you the results will be delicious. Beginners to the art of pastry-making will find the following guide-lines helpful:

1 Most of these cakes and pastries are based on one (occasionally more) of the pastries on pages 89–90 at the beginning of the chapter. Master them and you're halfway there. Choux and puff pastry are particularly useful and both are quite simple to make, though you will find that frozen or chilled puff pastry gives excellent results – almost as good as home made dough. See our note under the recipe on puff pastry to give you some idea of the quantities needed. You will see the home made gives more pastry than is needed for some recipes. This is because it really isn't practical to make puff pastry in smaller quantities – store the unused portion in the refrigerator or in the freezer until required.

2 Don't grudge the time needed to make such impressive recipes. Half an hour before the children get home is not the time to embark on a Gâteau Saint-Honoré. Reserve your talents for the really special occasions on which they will be properly appreciated.

3 Assemble your wits and your equipment before you start. Don't make do with improvised equipment if you want to get a truly professional finish.

4 Read the recipe right through before you start – preferably twice.

Basic pastries

Shortcrust pastry

250 g (9 oz) plain flour
pinch of salt
125 g (4½ oz) fat – half lard, half block
margarine or butter
about 45 ml (9 tsp) water

Mix the flour and salt together. Cut the fat into small knobs and add it. Using both hands, rub the fat into the flour between finger and thumb tips. After 2–3 minutes there will be no lumps of fat left and the mixture will look like fresh breadcrumbs. So far as possible add the water altogether sprinkling it evenly over the surface (uneven addition may cause blistering when the pastry is cooked), stirring with a round-bladed knife until the mixture begins to stick together in large lumps. With one hand, collect it together and knead lightly for a few seconds, to give a firm, smooth dough. The pastry can be used straight away, but is better if left to 'rest' for at least 15 minutes. It can also be wrapped in polythene and kept in the refrigerator for a day or two. Do allow to return to room temperature before using. When the pastry is required, sprinkle a very little flour on a working surface and on the rolling pin, but not on the pastry, roll out the dough evenly in one direction, turning it occasionally. The usual thickness is about 0.3 cm (⅛ in); don't pull or stretch it. Use as required. The usual oven temperature is 200°–220°C (400°–425°F) mark 6–7.

Pâte sucrée (sugar pastry)

This quantity will line a 23.5-cm (9-in) loose-bottomed fluted flan tin or about twenty-four tartlet cases.

200 g (7 oz) plain flour
pinch of salt
100 g (3½ oz) caster sugar
100 g (3½ oz) butter
3–4 egg yolks

Sift the flour with the salt into a pyramid on a working surface. Make a 'well' in the centre of the pyramid and put in the sugar. Cut the butter into pieces and add with the egg yolks to the sugar. Using a palette knife, flip the flour from side to side over the yolks and then pinch mixture together with the finger tips of one hand until all the flour is incorporated. Work dough

quickly and lightly into a smooth pastry, using the 'heel' of the hand, then form into a small ball, wrap in polythene and leave in the refrigerator or cool place for one hour. The usual oven temperature is 200°C (400°F) mark 6.

Flaky pastry

200 g (7 oz) plain flour
pinch of salt
150 g (5 oz) butter, or a mixture of butter or
block margarine and lard
about 105 ml (7 tbsp) cold water to mix
squeeze of lemon juice

Mix together the flour and salt. Soften the fat with the flat side of a palette knife, then divide into four equal sections. Rub one quarter of the softened fat into the flour. Mix to a soft, elastic dough with the water and lemon juice. On a floured surface, roll the pastry into an oblong three times as long as it is wide. Flake another quarter of the fat over the top two thirds of the pastry. Fold the bottom third up and the top third down and give the pastry half a turn so that the folds are now at the sides. Seal the edges of the pastry by pressing with the rolling pin, then re-roll as before and continue until all the fat is used up. Wrap loosely in greaseproof paper and leave to 'rest' in a refrigerator or cool place for at least 30 minutes before using. (This makes the handling and shaping of the pastry easier and gives a more evenly flaked texture.) Roll out and use as required. The usual oven temperature is 220°C (425°F) mark 7.

Choux pastry

50 g (2 oz) butter or block margarine
about 150 ml (¼ pint) water
120 ml (8 level tbsp) plain flour, sifted
2 eggs, lightly beaten

Melt the fat in the water and bring to the boil; remove from the heat and quickly tip the flour all at once Beat with a wooden spoon until the paste is smooth and forms a ball in the centre of the pan. (Take care not to over-beat or the mixture becomes fatty.) Allow to cool for a minute or two. Beat in the eggs a little at a time, beating vigorously – this is important – to trap in as much air as possible. A hand-held electric mixer is ideal for this and will also enable you to incorporate all the egg easily. Carry on beating until a sheen is visible. Use as required. The usual oven temperature is 200°–220°C (400°–425°F) mark 6–7.

When beating by hand with a wooden spoon the arms tend to tire, the beating speed is reduced and the final consistency is often too slack to retain its shape. In this case a little of the egg may have to be omitted.

Puff pastry

Puff pastry can be bought chilled or frozen and gives very good results. Buy a 368-g (13-oz) packet of frozen puff pastry to replace the quantities given below or a 212-g (7½-oz) packet when making recipes using half the quantity. Roll out bought puff pastry thinly. The recipes using puff pastry use half the quantities given below (it is impractical to make smaller amounts of the basic pastry). The best results are obtained when using strong plain flour.

If time allows, prepare the pastry the day before it is needed, giving it three rollings on one day; cover with greaseproof paper and a cloth or plastic bag and leave in the refrigerator overnight. The next day give it three more rollings and leave it to rest for 30 minutes before shaping.

200 g (7 oz) plain flour
pinch of salt
200 g (7 oz) unsalted butter
about 105 ml (7 tbsp) iced water

Sift together the flour and salt. Rub in half the butter and mix to a soft dough with cold water. Knead the dough lightly and shape into a round. Cut through half the depth in the form of a cross. Open out the flaps and roll out, keeping the centre four times as thick as the flaps. Place the second half of the butter (which should be firm, but not hard) in the centre of the dough, and fold over the flaps, envelope style, ending with the raw edge on the left-hand side. Press gently with a rolling-pin and roll into an oblong about 40.5 × 20.5 cm (16 × 8 in). Fold into three as for flaky pastry. Wrap in cling film and leave in a refrigerator or cool place for 30 minutes. Repeat this process five times. If you wish to freeze the pastry, divide in two, wrap in foil, overwrap in freezer wrap and freeze until required (*see page 119*). The usual oven temperature is 230°C (450°F) mark 8.

Custard tarts

½ recipe quantity shortcrust pastry (*see page 89*)
300 ml (½ pint) milk
15 g (½ oz) sugar
2 eggs
grated nutmeg

Lightly grease twelve deep patty tins. Roll out the pastry thinly and use to line the patty tins, pressing it firmly into them to exclude any air. Warm the milk to blood heat. add the sugar to the eggs and mix well together, until the egg white is no longer stringy, but avoid over-beating. Pour the milk on to the eggs, stirring. Strain the mixture into a jug and two-thirds fill each lined patty tin. Grate a little nutmeg over the top of each. Bake in the centre of the oven 190°C (375°F) mark 5, for 15 minutes, reduce the heat to 180°C (350°F) mark 4, and continue to cook until the custard is set and the pastry crisp.
MAKES 12

Cheesecake

450 g (1 lb) curd cheese
142 ml (¼ pint) carton double cream
75 g (3 oz) caster sugar
grated rind of 1 lemon
15 ml (1 tbsp) lemon juice
40 g (1½ oz) cornflour
2 eggs, beaten
¼ quantity shortcrust pastry (*see page 89*)
50 g (2 oz) seedless raisins

Sieve the curd cheese (or put it in an electric blender) and mix it with the cream; add the sugar, lemon rind and juice and the cornflour. Beat in the egg a little at a time.

Line the base and 0.5 cm (¼ in) up the sides of a loose-bottomed 20.5-cm (8-in) sandwich tin with a round of thinly rolled pastry; prick the base. Roll out the trimmings and cut into thin strips. Bake the pastry round in the oven at 190°C (375°F) mark 5, for 20 minutes. Cover the round with a layer of raisins, then spoon in the cheese mixture. Make a lattice over the filling with the pastry strips. Reduce the oven temperature to 180°C (350°F) mark 4, and bake the cheesecake in the oven for about 35 minutes, until the filling is just set. Leave the cake in the oven until cold. Place on an upturned basin to remove sides.

Eclairs

1 recipe quantity of choux pastry (*see page 89*)
142 ml ($\frac{1}{4}$ pint) carton double cream
1 egg white
chocolate or coffee glacé icing (*see page 72*)
   based on about 100 g (4 oz) icing sugar

Lightly grease two baking sheets. Put a 1-cm ($\frac{1}{2}$-in) plain vegetable nozzle inside a nylon or similar piping bag, turn back the bag to form a deep cuff, and spoon the choux paste in. Fold the bag over, pushing the mixture slowly down into the nozzle; fold the end over carefully.

On the two greased baking sheets pipe éclairs 6.5 cm (2$\frac{1}{2}$ in) long. Hold the bag at an angle after piping an éclair and trim off from the pipe with a knife.

Bake in the oven at 220°C (425°F) mark 7, for 20–25 minutes until well-risen and pale golden brown. The insides should be hollow and fairly dry.

Make a slit in the side of each éclair with the tip of a knife. Cool on a wire rack. When cold, and shortly before they are required, whip the cream and egg white together. Place a plain nozzle in a piping bag, fill with cream. Pipe a small amount of cream into each éclair.

Make the glacé icing and pour it into a shallow dish. When it is cool, stir, then dip in the filled éclairs, drawing each one across the surface of the icing, and lifting to release the icing. Leave to set.

Storing choux paste cases Eclairs and profiteroles can be stored, unfilled, for 24 hours or so in an airtight tin – refresh in the oven before using and cool on a wire rack.

ECLAIRS

1   *Trimming off the piped éclair with a knife*
2   *Coating with glacé icing*
3   *Finished éclair*

Cream buns

The characteristic light, crisp texture and crazy-paving tops of cream buns are achieved by baking the pastry in its own steam, and for this you will need a large, shallow tin with a tight-fitting lid. If this type of tin is not available, use a heavy, flat baking sheet and invert a roasting tin over it.

1 recipe quantity of choux pastry (*see page 89*)
284 ml ($\frac{1}{2}$ pint) carton double cream
icing sugar

Pipe the choux paste into small rounds on the tin, using a 1-cm ($\frac{1}{2}$-in) nozzle and leaving plenty of space between them. Cover and bake in the oven for 40–50 minutes at 200°C (400°F) mark 6. It is important that the buns are left undisturbed during the cooking, or the steam will escape and cause the buns to collapse. The end of the cooking time can be estimated by giving the tin a gentle shake – if the buns are ready, they will rattle on the base. Cool on a wire rack. Just before the buns are required, make a hole in the base of each. Whip the cream and fill the buns, piping with a small plain vegetable nozzle. Dust with icing sugar.
MAKES ABOUT 16

Profiteroles

1 recipe quantity of choux pastry (*see page 89*)
142 ml ($\frac{1}{4}$ pint) carton double cream
1 egg white
icing sugar

For the chocolate sauce
100 g (4 oz) chocolate dots
15 g ($\frac{1}{2}$ oz) butter
30 ml (2 tbsp) water
30 ml (2 tbsp) golden syrup
vanilla essence

Lightly grease baking sheets. Put a 1-cm ($\frac{1}{2}$-in) plain vegetable nozzle into a piping bag and pipe the choux paste on to the baking sheet in small bun shapes; hold the pipe upright while piping and lift it away with a sharp pull to release the mixture. Bake in the oven at 220°C (425°F) mark 7 for about 25 minutes until well-risen and golden brown. The insides should be hollow and fairly dry. Make a hole in the base of each bun with the tip of a knife or a skewer. Cool on a wire rack. When they are cold and shortly before required, make the sauce (see below) and prepare the cream (*see Eclairs, page 91*); fill the buns with cream, using a piping bag. Serve dusted with icing sugar, and with the chocolate sauce either spooned over or served separately.

To make the chocolate sauce Melt the chocolate dots with the butter in a small pan over a very low heat. Add the water, syrup and 2–3 drops of vanilla essence; stir well until smooth and well blended.
MAKES ABOUT 20

Gâteau Saint-Honoré

For the pastry base
100 g (4 oz) plain flour
pinch of salt
50 g (2 oz) butter, at room temperature
25 g (1 oz) caster sugar
1 egg yolk
1.25 ml ($\frac{1}{4}$ tsp) vanilla essence

For the choux ring and balls
1 recipe quantity of choux pastry (*see page 89*)
142 ml ($\frac{1}{4}$ pint) carton double cream

For the glaze
225 g (8 oz) sugar
120 ml (8 tbsp) water

For the pastry cream
568 ml (1 pint) milk
100 g (4 oz) caster sugar
50 g (2 oz) plain flour
15 g ($\frac{1}{2}$ oz) cornflour
2 large eggs
50 g (2 oz) butter

For the decoration
822-g (1 lb 13-oz) can of apricot halves, drained
angelica

Grease three baking sheets. For the pastry base, sift flour and salt on to a working surface. Make a well in the centre, add butter and sugar and work with fingers. Add the egg yolk and vanilla essence and mix to a soft dough, using the heel of one hand. Wrap and chill to a manageable consistency. Roll out the pastry into a round 22 cm ($8\frac{1}{2}$ in) in diameter on a floured surface. Place it on one baking sheet, prick the base with a fork, crimp the edge with the fingers and bake in the oven at 180°C (350°F) mark 4, for about 20 minutes. Cool on the baking sheet until beginning to firm, then lift carefully on to a wire rack.

Press the rim of a 22-cm ($8\frac{1}{2}$-in) cake tin on to the floured surface, then lift the cake tin on to the other baking sheet to make a floured circle. (Repeat the process if the flour ring is not sufficiently distinct.)

GATEAU SAINT-HONORÉ

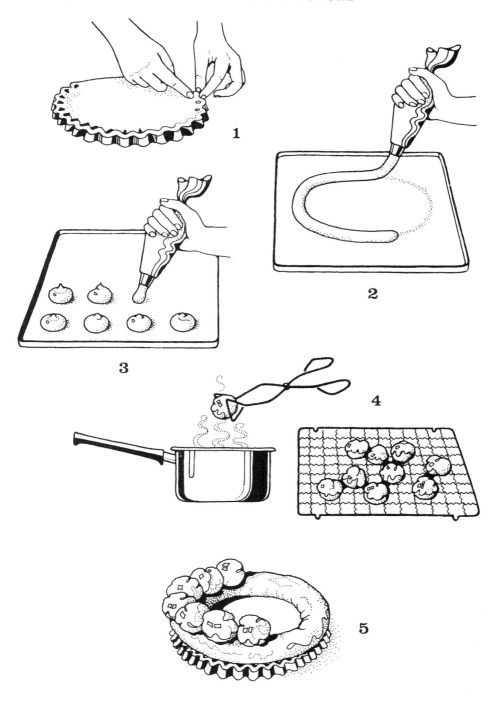

1 Crimping the edges of the pastry base with the fingers
2 Piping out a choux ring 3 Piping small choux buns of equal size
4 Using tongs to dip the choux buns in the glaze
5 Arranging the choux ring and buns on the pastry base

GATEAU SAINT HONORÉ
Finished cake

Spoon all the choux mixture into a forcing bag fitted with a large plain nozzle. With the floured ring as a guide, pipe two-thirds of the paste into a circle in one continuous movement, keeping the nozzle a little above the circle so that the paste falls evenly and smoothly. On the other greased baking sheet pipe sixteen small choux buns with the remaining paste in the bag. Bake the buns and the ring in the oven at 220°C (425°F) mark 7, for about 25 minutes. When the buns and rings are cooked, pierce the base of each. When cool and ready to use, fill the buns with whipped cream.

Make the glaze by dissolving the sugar in the water in a small pan and boiling rapidly until the thermometer reads 127°C (260°F) – or until a drop of syrup hardens when placed in cold water. Dip the top and sides of the cream-filled buns into the glaze with the aid of tongs. Put the pastry base on a flat serving plate, pour the remaining glaze over top of choux ring and carefully sit ring on base. Position the buns on the ring. Arrange all but six apricot halves in the centre of the gâteau. Top with warm pastry cream (see below), brush with apricot juice and finish with the remaining apricots and cut angelica. To finish off the gâteau, decorate pastry cream with diamonds of angelica.

To make the pastry cream heat the milk in a pan. Mix together the sugar, flour, cornflour and eggs and stir in a little of the hot milk. Return the mixture to the saucepan, stir and heat, stirring until the mixture thickens and just comes to the boil. Add the butter and beat well. Cover until required.

Cream horns

½ **recipe quantity of puff pastry** (*see page 90*)
1 **egg, beaten**
raspberry or blackcurrant jam
142 ml (¼ **pint) carton double cream**
75 ml (3 fl oz) **single cream**
icing sugar

Roll out the pastry to a strip 65 × 10 × 11.5 cm (26 × 4 × 4½ in). Brush with the beaten egg. Cut eight 1-cm (½-in) ribbons from the pastry with a sharp knife. Wind each round a cream horn tin, glazed side uppermost; start at the tip, overlapping 0.3 cm (⅛ in) and finish neatly on the underside. The pastry should not overlap the metal rim. Place on a dampened baking sheet, join-side down. Bake near the top of the oven for 8–10 minutes at 220°C (425°F) mark 7. Cool for a few minutes. Carefully twist in each tin, holding the pastry lightly in the other hand to ease it off the case. When cold, fill the tip of each horn with a little jam. Whip together the two creams, and fill the horns down to the jam. Dust with icing sugar.
MAKES 8 HORNS

CREAM HORNS

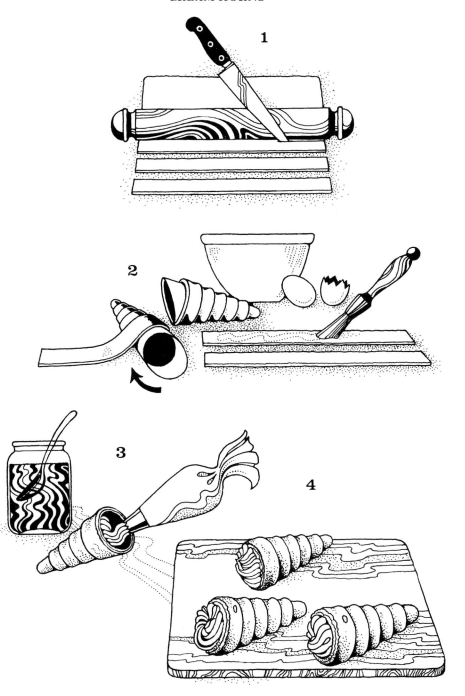

1   Cutting pastry into 1 cm ($\frac{1}{2}$ in) ribbons with sharp knife
2   Brushing and rolling cream horns
3   Filling a cream horn
4   Finished cream horns

PALMIERS

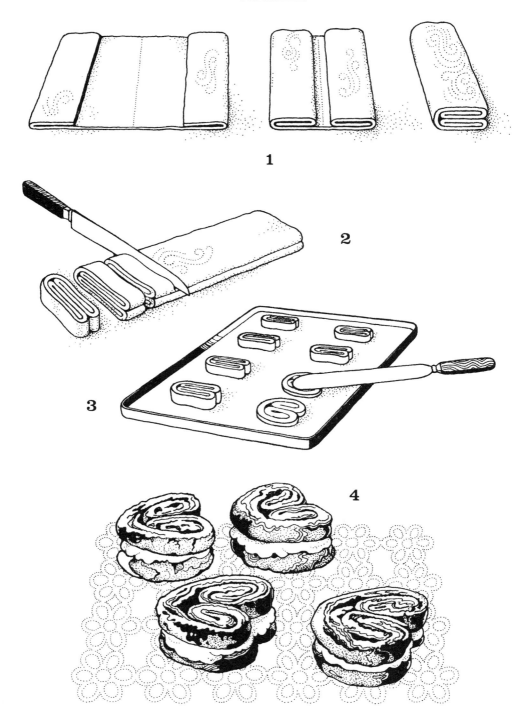

1   *How to fold palmiers*
2   *Cutting into 0.5 cm ($\frac{1}{4}$ in) slices*
3   *Flattening slightly with a palette knife*
4   *Finished palmiers*

Palmiers

½ recipe quantity of puff pastry (*see page 90*)
caster sugar
sweetened whipped cream or jam
icing sugar

Roll the pastry out evenly until it is 0.3 cm (⅛ in) thick
(0.2 cm (1/16 in) – if using bought pastry) and about
50 cm (20 in) long, sprinkle generously with caster
sugar. Fold the ends over halfway towards the centre
and press down firmly. Sprinkle generously with
more sugar and fold the sides to the centre again; press
and sprinkle with sugar. Place the two folded portions
together and press; then, with a sharp knife, cut into
0.5-cm (¼-in) slices. Place cut edge down on a damped
baking sheet, flatten slightly with a palette knife,
allowing room to spread, and bake in the oven at
220°C (425°F) mark 7, for 6–7 minutes, until golden
brown. Turn them and bake for a further 6–7
minutes. Cool on a rack and just before serving spread
sweetened whipped cream (or jam if preferred) on
half the slices, sandwich with the remaining slices and
dredge with icing sugar.

MAKES ABOUT 12

Mille-feuilles

COLOUR PLATE PAGE 80.

½ recipe quantity of puff pastry (*see page 90*)
100 g (4 oz) raspberry jam
284 ml (½ pint) carton double cream, whipped
175 g (6 oz) glacé icing (*see page 72*)
cochineal

Roll out the pastry into a rectangle 25.5 × 23 cm
(10 × 9 in) and prick well. Place on a dampened
baking sheet and bake in the oven at 230°C (450°F)
mark 8, for 25 minutes, until well-risen and golden-
brown. Cool on a rack. When cold, cut in half
lengthwise and spread the top of one piece with
raspberry jam; then cover with the whipped cream.
Make the glacé icing and mix 15 ml (1 tbsp) icing with
a few drops of cochineal to make a deep pink colour.
Pour this into a greaseproof paper piping bag (*see page
109*) cut tip off bag just before required. Spread the
white icing over the top of the pastry. With the pink
icing, pipe lines across the mille-feuilles 1 cm (½ in)
apart. Draw a skewer down the length of the mille-
feuilles at 1 cm (½ in) intervals to make the feathering.
Leave to set, then cut into pieces.

MAKES 6 SLICES

Sacristains

*Sacristains can be shaped in many ways. The strips
can be twisted, shaped into circles or tied into knots.
This is a good way of using up trimmings of puff or
flaky pastry. Knead them together very lightly, roll
out and continue as in the recipe.*

½ recipe quantity of puff pastry (*see page 90*)
1 egg white
25 g (1 oz) almonds, skinned and chopped
25 g (1 oz) caster sugar
7.5 ml (1½ level tsp) ground cinnamon

Roll out the pastry to an oblong 10 × 35.5 cm
(4 × 14 in). Brush the lightly beaten egg white over
the pastry to within 1 cm (½ in) of the edge. Sprinkle
with the nuts and mixed sugar and cinnamon. Cut the
pastry cross-ways to give strips 1 cm (½ in) wide and
10 cm (4 in) long. Place them on a dampened baking
sheet and bake towards the top of the oven for about 10
minutes at 220°C (425°F) mark 7.

MAKES 28

Danish pastries

The basic dough
25 g (1 oz) fresh yeast
about 150 ml (¼ pint) water
450 g (1 lb) plain flour (do not use strong flour
    for this recipe)
5 ml (1 level tsp) salt
50 g (2 oz) lard
30 ml (2 level tbsp) sugar
2 eggs, beaten
300 g (10 oz) butter
beaten egg to glaze

Blend the yeast with the water. Mix the flour and salt,
rub in the lard and stir in the sugar. Add the yeast
liquid and beaten eggs and mix to an elastic dough,
adding a little more water if necessary. Knead lightly.
Cover the bowl and leave the dough to 'rest' in a
refrigerator for 10 minutes. Work the butter with a
knife until soft and form it into an oblong. Roll out the
dough on a floured surface into an oblong about three
times the size of the butter, put the butter in the centre
of the dough and enclose it, overlapping the
unbuttered sides just across the middle and sealing
the open sides with a rolling pin.

Turn the dough so that the folds are to the sides and
roll into a strip three times as long as it is wide; fold the
bottom third up, and the top third down, cover and
leave to 'rest' for 10 minutes. Turn, repeat, rolling,

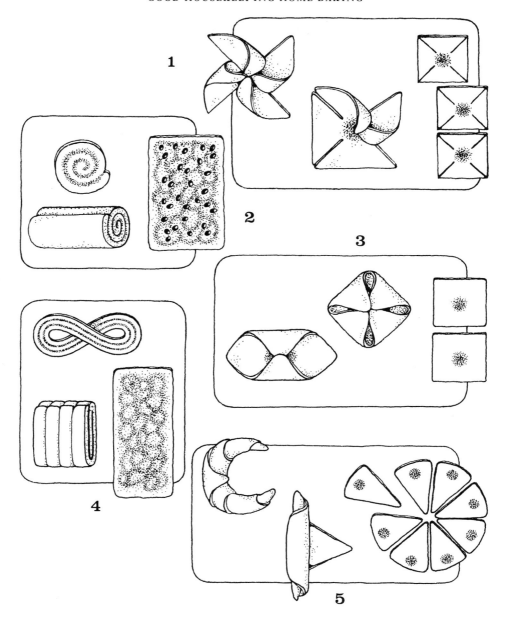

SHAPING DANISH PASTRIES

1 Imperial stars 2 Pinwheels 3 Cushions 4 Twists 5 Crescents

folding and 'resting' twice more, make into the shapes described on page 99 and fill with one of the fillings.

To finish Danish pastries
After shaping them (see above), prove for 20–30 minutes. Brush with beaten egg and bake in the oven at 220°C (425°F) mark 7, for about 15 minutes. While they are still hot, brush with thin white glacé icing (*see page 72*) and sprinkle with flaked or chopped almonds which have been lightly browned under the

grill. Finish the centres of imperial stars and cushions with a blob of pastry cream (*see this page*) or redcurrant jelly.

THE TRADITIONAL SHAPES

Crescents Roll out half of the dough thinly and cut out two 23-cm (9-in) rounds. Divide each into eight segments and put a little almond paste or pastry cream (*see this page*) mixture at the base of each. Roll up from the base and curl round to form a crescent.
MAKES 16 PASTRIES

Imperial stars Roll out half of the dough thinly, cut into 7.5-cm (3-in) squares and make diagonal cuts from each corner to within 1 cm ($\frac{1}{2}$ in) of the centre. Put a piece of almond paste in the centre of the square and fold one corner of each cut section down the centre, securing the tips with a little beaten egg.
MAKES ABOUT 16 PASTRIES

Cushions Using 7.5-cm (3-in) squares, put a little almond paste in the centre and either fold over two alternate corners to the centre or fold over all four corners, securing the tips with beaten egg.

Pinwheels Roll out half of the dough into two oblongs 30 cm (12 in) long and 20.5 cm (8 in) wide. Spread with cinnamon butter and sultanas, roll up like Swiss rolls, cut into 2.5-cm (1-in) slices and place cut side upwards on a baking sheet.
MAKES ABOUT 16 PASTRIES

Twists Roll out half dough as above. Cut each oblong lengthwise to give four pieces. Spread with cinnamon butter and fold the bottom third up and the top third down. Cut each across into thin slices. Twist these slices and put on a baking sheet.
MAKES ABOUT 16 PASTRIES

FILLINGS FOR DANISH PASTRIES

Almond paste

15 g ($\frac{1}{2}$ oz) butter
75 g (3 oz) caster sugar
75 g (3 oz) ground almonds
1 egg, beaten
almond essence (optional)

Cream the butter and sugar, stir in the almonds and add enough egg to make a soft spreading consistency; add a few drops of almond essence if you wish.

Confectioner's custard or pastry cream

1 whole egg, separated
1 egg yolk
50 g (2 oz) caster sugar
30 ml (2 level tbsp) plain flour
30 ml (2 level tbsp) cornflour
300 ml ($\frac{1}{2}$ pint) milk
vanilla essence

Cream the egg yolks and sugar together until really thick and pale in colour. Beat in the flour and cornflour and a little cold milk to make a smooth paste. Heat the rest of the milk in a saucepan until almost boiling and pour on to the egg mixture, stirring well all the time. Return the mixture to the saucepan and stir over a low heat until the mixture boils. Beat the egg white until stiff. Remove the custard mixture from the heat and fold in the egg white. Again return the pan to the heat, add essence to taste and cook for a further 2–3 minutes. Cool before using.

Cinnamon butter

50 g (2 oz) butter
50 g (2 oz) caster sugar
10 ml (2 level tsp) ground cinnamon

Cream the butter and sugar and beat in the cinnamon.

Genoese sponge

This is the basis for many gâteaux. It is lighter than the basic Victoria sandwich, has a pleasant butter taste and cuts well.

40 g 1$\frac{1}{2}$ oz) butter
75 g (2$\frac{1}{2}$ oz) plain flour
15 ml (1 level tbsp) cornflour
3 large eggs
75 g (3 oz) caster sugar

Grease and line two 18-cm (7-in) sandwich tins. Heat the butter gently until it is melted, remove it from the heat and let it stand for a few minutes, for the salt and any sediment to settle. Sift the flour and cornflour. Put the eggs and sugar in a large bowl, stand this over a saucepan of hot water and whisk until light and creamy – the mixture should be stiff enough to retain the impression of the whisk for a few seconds. Remove from heat and whisk until cool. (If you are using an electric mixer no heat is required during whisking.) Using a metal spoon, carefully fold in half the re-sifted flour, then fold in the melted butter (cooled until it just flows) poured round the edge of the mixture, taking care not to let the salt and sediment run in. Fold in the remaining flour carefully. Fold very lightly or the fat will sink to the bottom and make a heavy cake. Pour the mixture into the tins and bake in the oven at 190°C (375°F) mark 5, until golden brown and firm to the touch – 20–25 minutes. Turn out to cool on a wire rack. Fill and ice as desired (*see pages 71–75 for fillings and icings*).

Gâteau nougatine

For the cake
6 large eggs
175 g (6 oz) caster sugar
100 g (4 oz) plain flour
50 g (2 oz) cornflour
150–175 g (5–6 oz) butter, melted

For the filling
crème au beurre (*see page 71*)
10 ml (2 tsp) Tía Maria

For the nougat and topping
175 g (6 oz) caster sugar
100 g (4 oz) blanched almonds, finely chopped
1 lemon
30 ml (2 tbsp) apricot glaze (*see page 107*)
**175 g (6 oz) plain chocolate-flavoured cake
    covering**

Grease and base line two 23-cm (9-in) round sandwich tins. Make up the basic cake, following method for Genoese sponge on page 99. Bake the cakes one above the other in the oven at 220°C (425°F) mark 7, for 10 minutes, then reduce the temperature to 190°C (375°F) mark 5, and bake for a further 15 minutes. Turn out and cool on a wire rack. Meanwhile make up the creme au beurre, adding the Tía Maria.

For the nougat, put the sugar in a heavy-based pan and dissolve over a very low heat; when it is caramel-coloured, add the almonds a little at a time, stirring gently with a metal spoon. Turn quickly on to an oiled metal surface, then, using a whole lemon, thinly roll out the nougat. Using a warmed cutter, stamp out twelve to fourteen 'leaf' shapes. Leave the remainder of the nougat to set, then roughly crush it. (Should the nougat become too set before all the 'leaf' shapes are cut, pop it into a warm oven for a few minutes.)

To finish the cake sandwich the layers of Genoese together with some of the crème au beurre. Spread the remainder round the edge and coat evenly with crushed nougat. Brush the cake top with apricot glaze. Melt the chocolate covering and spread over the glaze, easing it to the edge with a knife. When it is nearly set, mark the chocolate surface into serving portions with a warmed knife. Arrange the nougat 'leaves' in position before the chocolate completely sets, or fix with a little crème au beurre.

Gâteau Armandine

125 g (4½ oz) caster sugar
3 large eggs
75 g (3 oz) plain flour

For the filling and decoration
apricot glaze (*see page 108*)
284 ml (½ pint) carton double cream
100 g (4 oz) whole blanched almonds
icing sugar

Grease and base-line a 24-cm (9½-in) – top measurement – moule à manqué (sloping-sided) cake tin. Whisk together the sugar and eggs until really thick and creamy – the whisk should leave a trail when lifted from the mixture. Sift the flour over the surface and lightly fold in with a metal spoon. Turn the mixture into the prepared tin and bake in the oven at 190°C (375°F) mark 5, for about 30 minutes, until well risen and golden brown. Turn out and cool on a wire rack.

When the cake is cold, split and sandwich with apricot glaze. Using a sharp knife, split the nuts in half and cut in thin slices. Whip the double cream and lightly sweeten with icing sugar. Completely mask the cake with the cream and cover with sliced nuts. Dust lightly with icing sugar and chill. Eat fresh.

Black Forest cake

3 eggs
125 g (4½ oz) caster sugar
75 g (3 oz) plain flour
15 g (½ oz) cocoa
284 ml (½ pint) carton double cream
142 ml (¼ pint) carton single cream
**425-g (15-oz) can cherries (Morellos for
    preference)**
10 ml (2 level tsp) arrowroot
kirsch
flaked chocolate bar

Grease a 23-cm (9-in) straight-sided sandwich tin and line the base and sides with greaseproof paper, the sideband to come 2.5 cm (1 in) above the edge.

Make a whisked sponge in the usual way with the eggs, sugar and flour, previously sifted with the cocoa (*see page 114*). Turn the mixture into the tin and bake in the oven at 190°C (375°F) mark 5, for 30 minutes, until well risen and just firm to the touch. Turn on to a rack. When completely cold, cut into three layers horizontally.

Whip together the double and single creams until soft peaks can be formed. Drain the cherries, reserve twelve whole ones, stone and halve the rest. Measure the juice and make up to 150 ml ($\frac{1}{4}$ pint) with water, if necessary. Thicken with arrowroot in the usual way; if liked, add some pink colouring before stirring in the halved cherries. Leave until cold. Layer up the cake with the cream and the halved cherry mixture, sprinkling each layer with a little kirsch. Completely mask the cake with the remaining cream, arrange the flaked chocolate in the centre and the whole cherries round the edge. Leave in a cool place for several hours for the flavours to blend.

Butterscotch gâteau

225 g (8 oz) plain flour
7.5 ml (1$\frac{1}{2}$ level tsp) baking powder
2.5 ml ($\frac{1}{2}$ level tsp) bicarbonate of soda
pinch of salt
225 g (8 oz) soft dark brown sugar
100 g (4 oz) butter
175 ml (6 fl oz) milk
7.5 ml (1$\frac{1}{2}$ tsp) vanilla essence
2 eggs, beaten

For the butter cream
100 g (4 oz) butter
30 ml (2 tbsp) black treacle
10 ml (2 tsp) lemon juice
225 g (8 oz) icing sugar, sifted

For the caramel
50 g (2 oz) caster sugar
60 ml (4 tbsp) water

Grease and base line a 20.5-cm (8-in) diameter 6.5-cm (2$\frac{1}{2}$-in) deep moule à manqué (sloping-sided) cake tin. Sift together the first four ingredients. Stir in the brown sugar. With an electric mixer cream the butter until soft and slowly add the dry ingredients until crumbly. Continue beating, adding the milk and

essence, for 2 minutes. Add the eggs, beat 1–2 minutes more. Pour into the prepared tin. Bake in the oven at 190°C (375°F), mark 5, for about 1 hour. Turn out and cool on a rack.

To make the butter cream, cream the butter, treacle and lemon juice together. Beat in the icing sugar.

Cut the cake in half and sandwich with some of the butter cream. Spread two-thirds more over the cake. Ridge the sides and top with a fork and pipe the rest of butter cream round the edge. Decorate with the caramel.

To make the caramel Dissolve the sugar in the water over a low heat. Boil to a caramel colour. Pour on to a greased tin. When set, break into small pieces.

Blackcurrant and chocolate gâteau

225 g (8 oz) plain flour
50 g (2 oz) cornflour
50 g (2 oz) cocoa
20 ml (4 level tsp) baking powder
2.5 ml ($\frac{1}{2}$ level tsp) salt
4 eggs, separated
275 g (10 oz) caster sugar
200 ml (7 fl oz) corn oil
200 ml (7 fl oz) water
425-g (15-oz) can blackcurrants
10 ml (2 level tsp) arrowroot
284 ml ($\frac{1}{2}$ pint) carton double cream
30 ml (2 tbsp) rum, optional
chocolate curls (see below)
icing sugar for dredging

Lightly oil and base line two 23-cm (9-in) sandwich tins. Sift first five ingredients into a bowl. Whisk egg yolks, sugar, oil, water, stir into dry ingredients and beat well. Whisk egg whites until stiff and fold in lightly. Divide mixture between tins, bake at 190°C (375°F) mark 5 for about 30 minutes; turn out and cool on a wire rack.

Drain blackcurrants, reserve juice and blend a little with the arrowroot. Stir in remaining juice, bring to the boil and boil for 1 minute. Let it cool before spreading this glaze on top of each cake. Whip cream with rum and use with blackcurrants to sandwich the cakes. Make curls from a softened bar of chocolate with a potato peeler; chill until firm. Decorate cake top and dredge with icing sugar.

Orange liqueur gâteau

two 19-cm (7-in) round Genoese sponge cakes
(*see page 99*)
30–45 ml (2–3 tbsp) Grand Marnier
grated rind of 1 orange
284 ml ($\frac{1}{2}$ pint) carton double cream, whipped
chopped walnuts
15–30 ml (1–2 tbsp) fresh orange juice
150 g (5 oz) icing sugar, sifted
thin slices of fresh orange

Sprinkle each round of cake with Grand Marnier.
Add the orange rind to the cream and use about half of
the mixture to sandwich the two cakes together.
Spread a little of it round the sides and roll the cake in
the chopped walnuts. Add sufficient orange juice to
the sugar to make an icing thick enough to coat the
back of a spoon and spread this over the top of the
cake. When the icing is set, pipe with whirls of cream
and decorate with thin slices of orange. Keep in cool
place, eat preferably on day of making.

Devil's food cake

*This cake was first made in the United States, where
it is usually eaten today as a dessert.*

450 g (1 lb) plain flour
15 ml (3 level tsp) bicarbonate of soda
pinch of salt
75 g (3 oz) cocoa
345 ml ($\frac{1}{2}$ pint + 3 tbsp) milk
10 ml (2 tsp) vanilla essence
150 g (5 oz) butter
400 g (14 oz) soft brown sugar
4 eggs, beaten

For the American frosting and decoration
700 g (1$\frac{1}{2}$ lb) caster sugar
180 ml ($\frac{1}{4}$ pint plus 2 tbsp) water
3 egg whites
1 oz plain chocolate, optional

Grease three 22-cm (8$\frac{1}{2}$-in) straight-sided sandwich
tins and line with greaseproof paper. Sift together the
flour, bicarbonate of soda and salt. Mix together the
cocoa, milk and vanilla essence until smooth. Using
an electric hand mixer, cream the butter until pale in
colour, then gradually beat in the sugar. Add the eggs
one at a time, beating very thoroughly after each has
been added. When all the eggs are added, beat in the
flour and cocoa mixtures alternately until all is added.
Divide the mixture between the tins. Place two cakes

on the top shelf and one on the lower. Bake in the oven
at 180°C (350°F) mark 4, for about 35 minutes, until
firm to the touch. Turn on to a wire rack and cool.

Put the sugar for the frosting in a pan with the
water, dissolve over a low heat then boil rapidly to
115°C (240°F) (use a sugar thermometer). Meanwhile
beat the egg whites in a large deep bowl until stiff.
Allow the bubbles in the syrup to settle, then slowly
pour the hot syrup on to the egg whites, beating
constantly. Once all the sugar syrup is added,
continue beating until the mixture stands in peaks and
just starts to become matt round the edges – the icing
sets quickly, so work rapidly. Sandwich the three
cakes together with a little of the frosting. Spread the
remaining frosting over the cake with a palette knife.
Pull the icing up into peaks all over, then leave the cake
on a cooling rack for 30 minutes, to allow the icing to
set slightly. Place the chocolate in a small basin and
stand it in a pan of hot water over a low heat until
melted. Dribble the chocolate over the top of the cake
with a teaspoon.

Whisky spice cake

*This cake is lightly crumbed and is to be eaten with a
fork.*

225 g (8 oz) seedless raisins
water
125 g (4 oz) butter
150 g (5 oz) soft brown sugar
1 large egg
175 g (6 oz) plain flour
5 ml (1 level tsp) bicarbonate of soda
2.5 ml ($\frac{1}{2}$ level tsp) ground cloves
2.5 ml ($\frac{1}{2}$ level tsp) ground nutmeg
100 g (4 oz) walnut halves, chopped
30 ml (2 tbsp) whisky

For the butter cream
75 g (3 oz) butter
1 egg yolk
225 g (8 oz) icing sugar
15 ml (1 tbsp) whisky

For the decoration
25 g (1 oz) walnut halves
icing sugar

Grease and line two 20.5-cm (8-in) straight-sided
sandwich tins. Put raisins and 150 ml ($\frac{1}{4}$ pint) water in
a small saucepan, cover and simmer for 15 minutes.
Drain the liquid and make up to 150 ml ($\frac{1}{4}$ pint) with
more water. Cream butter and sugar until light and

fluffy. Beat in the egg. Sift flour, bicarbonate of soda and spices over the creamed mixture and fold in with the raisin liquid. Add walnut halves, drained raisins and whisky. Mix well. Divide equally between prepared tins. Bake in the oven at 180°C (350°F) mark 4, for about 35 minutes. Turn out carefully and cool on a wire rack.

To make the butter cream, beat the butter, gradually beat in the egg yolk, sifted icing sugar and whisky until light and fluffy. Sandwich the cake together with butter cream filling. Decorate with sifted icing sugar and walnut halves.

Coffee almond layer

5 large eggs
30 ml (2 tbsp) coffee essence
150 g (5 oz) caster sugar
125 g (4 oz) plain flour
25 g (1 oz) cornflour

For the butter cream
225 g (8 oz) unsalted butter
30 ml (2 tbsp) dark rum
275 g (10 oz) icing sugar

For the decoration
125 g (4 oz) flaked almonds, toasted
instant coffee powder

Grease and line two 21.5-cm (8½-in) sandwich tins. In a deep bowl over a pan of hot but not boiling water, whisk eggs, coffee essence and caster sugar until pale and really thick. Cool away from heat. Sift the flours together and then re-sift over the egg mixture. Using a metal spoon, fold in flour using a figure of eight movement. Divide between the two tins. Bake in the oven at 190°C (375°F) mark 5, for about 25 minutes. Leave in tins 5 minutes. Turn out on to wire rack to cool.

Cream butter, gradually beat in rum and sifted icing sugar. Sandwich coffee sponges together with some of the butter cream and use the rest to mask the cake completely. Press almonds into the butter cream. Dredge with icing sugar. Cover top with a piece of paper with a 7.5-cm (3-in) circle cut from the centre. Sprinkle instant coffee over the hole and carefully remove paper.

Linzertorte

150 g (5 oz) plain flour
2.5 ml (½ level tsp) ground cinnamon
75 g (3 oz) butter
50 g (2 oz) caster sugar
50 g (2 oz) ground almonds
grated rind of 1 lemon
2 egg yolks
15 ml (1 tbsp) lemon juice
350 g (12 oz) raspberry jam or fresh or frozen raspberries (see below)*
whipped double cream for serving

Sift the flour and cinnamon into a bowl and rub in the butter. Add the sugar, ground almonds and the lemon rind. Beat the egg yolks and add with the lemon juice to the flour, to make a stiff dough. Knead lightly and leave in a cool place for 30 minutes. Roll out two-thirds of the pastry and use to line a 21.5-cm (8½-in) fluted flan ring on a baking sheet. Fill with raspberry jam. Roll out the remaining pastry and cut into 1-cm (½-in) strips with a pastry wheel. Use to make a lattice design over the jam. Bake in the oven at 190°C (375°F) mark 5, for 25–30 minutes. Allow to cool, remove from the flan ring and serve with whipped cream.

* If using fresh or frozen raspberries in place of the jam: put 450 g (1 lb) raspberries with 15 ml (1 tbsp) water and a knob of butter in a pan, add a little sugar to taste and boil to reduce to a thick purée. Cool before using.

The Celebration Cake

There is bound to be an occasion in your life when you will have to turn your hand to making and decorating that extra special celebration cake. Whether it's a birthday, christening, anniversary or even a wedding, don't be daunted – if you follow our step by step instructions in this chapter you won't go wrong, and your family and friends will much appreciate the special taste of home baking, even if the decoration isn't quite as spectacular as a professional patissière's.

Following the step by step instructions for making the actual cake there are charts to show at a glance how much of each ingredient is needed for different tin sizes, and how to adjust quantities for different shapes of tin. We show you how to cover the cake with almond paste, how to ice it and put on the finishing touches – and just for good measure we have included two slightly less rich basic fruit cakes as alternatives. Make the cake well in advance to give it time to mature: rich fruit cakes positively improve with 2–3 months storage if they are carefully wrapped in aluminium foil and stored in an airtight tin. To avoid last minute panics, allow yourself plenty of time to complete the decoration. When the cake has been flat iced, work out a simple design – if you're planning something ambitious you'll find it a help to draw a rough plan on a piece of greaseproof paper – and pipe it on with a piping bag. If it's a Christmas cake you're decorating, make a 'snow scene' with royal icing – look at the picture on page 81 to see just how effective it is. Another simple decoration can be made with sugared flowers: just wash and dry the flowers, (open petalled flowers such as primroses, violets, daisies, are particularly effective), paint the petals with egg white and dust them with caster sugar; leave them until dry before arranging.

INGREDIENT QUANTITIES AND TIN SIZES FOR RICH FRUIT CELEBRATION CAKES

Formal cakes are usually based on a rich fruit mixture, covered with almond paste and iced with royal icing. Below we give a chart showing how much fruit mixture is needed for cakes of all shapes and sizes, and ingredient quantities to make up the required weight. Figures quoted at the top of each column give the tin size measured across the top.

SIZE OF SQUARE TIN:		15 cm *(6 in)* square	18 cm *(7 in)* square	20.5 cm *(8 in)* square	23 cm *(9 in)* square	25.5 cm *(10 in)* square	28 cm *(11 in)* square	30.5 cm *(12 in)* square
SIZE OF ROUND TIN:	15 cm *(6 in)* round	18 cm *(7 in)* round	20.5 cm *(8 in)* round	23 cm *(9 in)* round	25.5 cm *(10 in)* round	28 cm *(11 in)* round	30.5 cm *(12 in)* round	–
Currants	225 g *(8 oz)*	350 g *(12 oz)*	450 g *(1 lb)*	625 g *(1 lb 6 oz)*	775 g *(1 lb 12 oz)*	1.1 kg *(2 lb 8 oz)*	1.5 kg *(3 lb 2 oz)*	1.7 kg *(3 lb 12 oz)*
Sultanas	100 g *(3½ oz)*	125 g *(4½ oz)*	200 g *(7 oz)*	225 g *(8 oz)*	375 g *(13 oz)*	400 g *(14 oz)*	525 g *(1 lb 3 oz)*	625 g *(1 lb 6 oz)*
Raisins	100 g *(3½ oz)*	125 g *(4½ oz)*	200 g *(7 oz)*	225 g *(8 oz)*	375 g *(13 oz)*	400 g *(14 oz)*	525 g *(1 lb 3 oz)*	625 g *(1 lb 6 oz)*
Glacé cherries	50 g *(2 oz)*	75 g *(3 oz)*	150 g *(5 oz)*	175 g *(6 oz)*	250 g *(9 oz)*	275 g *(10 oz)*	350 g *(12 oz)*	425 g *(15 oz)*
Mixed peel	25 g *(1 oz)*	50 g *(2 oz)*	75 g *(3 oz)*	100 g *(4 oz)*	150 g *(5 oz)*	200 g *(7 oz)*	250 g *(9 oz)*	275 g *(10 oz)*
Almonds	25 g *(1 oz)*	50 g *(2 oz)*	75 g *(3 oz)*	100 g *(4 oz)*	150 g *(5 oz)*	200 g *(7 oz)*	250 g *(9 oz)*	275 g *(10 oz)*
Lemon rind	a little	a little	a little	¼ lemon	¼ lemon	½ lemon	½ lemon	1 lemon
Plain flour	175 g *(6 oz)*	200 g *(7½ oz)*	350 g *(12 oz)*	400 g *(14 oz)*	600 g *(1 lb 5 oz)*	700 g *(1 lb 8 oz)*	825 g *(1 lb 13 oz)*	1 kg *(2 lb 6 oz)*
Mixed spice	1.25 ml *(¼ level tsp)*	2.5 ml *(½ level tsp)*	2.5 ml *(½ level tsp)*	5 ml *(1 level tsp)*	5 ml *(1 level tsp)*	10 ml *(2 level tsp)*	12.5 ml *(2½ level tsp)*	12.5 ml *(2½ level tsp)*
Cinnamon	1.25 ml *(¼ level tsp)*	2.5 ml *(½ level tsp)*	2.5 ml *(½ level tsp)*	5 ml *(1 level tsp)*	5 ml *(1 level tsp)*	10 ml *(2 level tsp)*	12.5 ml *(2½ level tsp)*	12.5 ml *(2½ level tsp)*
Butter	150 g *(5 oz)*	175 g *(6 oz)*	275 g *(10 oz)*	350 g *(12 oz)*	500 g *(1 lb 2 oz)*	600 g *(1 lb 5 oz)*	800 g *(1 lb 12 oz)*	950 g *(2 lb 2 oz)*
Sugar	150 g *(5 oz)*	175 g *(6 oz)*	275 g *(10 oz)*	350 g *(12 oz)*	500 g *(1 lb 2 oz)*	600 g *(1 lb 5 oz)*	800 g *(1 lb 12 oz)*	950 g *(2 lb 2 oz)*
Large eggs	2½	3	5	6	9	11	14	17
Brandy	15 ml *(1 tbsp)*	15 ml *(1 tbsp)*	15–30 ml *(1–2 tbsp)*	30 ml *(2 tbsp)*	30–45 ml *(2–3 tbsp)*	45 ml *(3 tbsp)*	60 ml *(4 tbsp)*	90 ml *(6 tbsp)*
Baking time (approx)	2½–3 hrs	3 hrs	3½ hrs	4 hrs	6 hrs	7 hrs	8 hrs	8½ hrs
Weight of cake when cooked	1.1 kg *(2½ lb)*	1.6 kg *(3¼ lb)*	2.2 kg *(4¾ lb)*	2.7 kg *(6 lb)*	4 kg *(9 lb)*	5.2 kg *(11½ lb)*	6.7 kg *(14¾ lb)*	7.7 kg *17 lb*

Quantities of almond and royal icing for celebration cakes

SIZE OF SQUARE TIN		15 cm (6 in) square	18 cm (7 in) square	20.5 cm (8 in) square	23 cm (9 in) square	25.5 cm (10 in) square	28 cm (11 in) square	30.5 cm (12 in) square
SIZE OF ROUND TIN	15 cm (6 in) round	18 cm (7 in) round	20.5 cm (8 in) round	23 cm (9 in) round	25.5 cm (10 in) round	28 cm (11 in) round	30.5 cm (12 in) round	–
Almond paste	350 g (¾ lb)	450 g (1 lb)	550 g (1¼ lb)	800 g (1¾ lb)	900 g (2 lb)	1 kg (2¼ lb)	1.1 kg (2½ lb)	1.4 kg (3 lb)
Royal icing	450 g (1 lb)	550 g (1¼ lb)	700 g (1½ lb)	900 g (2 lb)	1 kg (2¼ lb)	1.1 kg (2½ lb)	1.4 kg (3 lb)	1.6 kg (3½ lb)

Step by step method of making a rich fruit celebration cake

1 Prepare the tins (see *page 114*).
2 Wash and thoroughly dry the currants and sultanas (unless you are using pre-washed packaged fruit). *See page 120.*
3 Chop the stoned raisins. Peel, blanch and chop the sweet almonds. Quarter the glacé cherries.
4 Sift together the flour and spices. Add the grated lemon rind.
5 Cream the butter and gradually beat in the sugar until light and fluffy.
6 Beat in the beaten eggs a little at a time. If the mixture begins to curdle, beat in 15–30 ml (1–2 level tbsp) flour.
7 Fold in the rest of the flour then the fruit, nuts and brandy. The dark colouring of a cake is given by long, slow cooking, but if you prefer an even darker colour, add a few drops of ready-prepared gravy browning. Added colouring is useful for top tiers, which are inclined to be paler since they take relatively less time to cook.
8 Spoon the mixture into the prepared tin and level the surface. Hollow out the centre of the cake slightly, so that it will be level when cooked. At this stage the mixture may be left overnight. Cover lightly with a cloth and leave in a cool place.
9 Bake on the lowest shelf in the oven at 150°C (300°F) mark 2, for the time stated on the chart. Look at the cake half-way through the cooking time. If it seems to be browning too quickly cover the top with a double thickness of greaseproof paper. With large cakes, in particular, it is often wise to reduce the heat to 140°C (275°F) mark ½–1, after two-thirds of the cooking time.

10 Cool the cake in the tin for at least an hour before turning out on to a wire rack. When it is cold, prick at intervals with a fine skewer and spoon some brandy evenly over the whole surface.
11 Wrap completely in greaseproof paper and then in kitchen foil. Store for at least a month – preferably 2–3 months in a cool, dry place.

Cake boards
Thick silver cake boards: often called 'drums' by confectioners and at the stationery shops that sell them. Round or square, they should be large enough to project 2.5 cm (1 in) all round the cake – that is 5 cm (2 in) larger than the cake. Sometimes, however, the large base cake looks well with a board that is 7.5 cm (3 in) larger and a small top tier with a board only 2.5 cm (1 in) larger.

Design and finish
Plan the design for your cake well in advance. Make applied decorations at least two days before fixing them to the iced cake preferably complete all *decorating* a week before the cake is needed but don't assemble the tiers (if you are using them) until the very last possible moment.

When you have planned the design – and the simplest can be very effective – draw the pattern on greaseproof paper the same size as the top of the cake. Then put the paper on the top surface and prick out the key points on to the icing. Make, in advance, the required number of applied decorations like sugar flowers, plaques or initials and have ready-to-hand any bought decorations – silver leaves, heather, horseshoes, etc – that you wish to add. It's a good idea, unless you're very experienced, to practise piped designs – lines, trellis, scrolls, borders (*see page 110*) – on a flat surface or an upturned plate before actually piping them on to the cake. After completing the piped design, arrange sugar flowers and other decorations in place, finally fixing them with a little icing when you are satisfied with the effect.

The position of pillars should be established when the design is being planned, but the pillars themselves are best fixed in position at the end, otherwise they will hinder piping. A thin royal-iced cake board may be put on the iced surface of the bottom tier, to take the pressure of the pillars; a ring of piped decoration hides its edge. This should not be necessary if the basic coats have been hardened sufficiently.

The almond paste

This should be put on a week before the first coat of royal icing. The cake should have an even top, but if necessary the surface can be levelled with a sharp knife; alternatively, use the flat base of the cake as the top. After applying the almond paste, put the cake aside on a clean board, cover it loosely with greaseproof paper and leave to dry out.

How to apply almond paste

1 Make up the required amount of paste.
2 With a piece of string or strong thread measure round the outer edge of the cake.
3 Take two-thirds of the almond paste and roll it on a surface dredged with icing sugar or between non-stick paper to a rectangle half the length of the string and twice the depth of the cake in width. Trim with a knife and halve lengthwise. Knead the trimmings into the remaining paste and roll out to fit the cake top.
4 Brush the sides of the cake with apricot glaze. Put the two strips of almond paste round the cake and smooth the joins with a round-bladed knife, keeping the top and bottom edges square.
5 Brush the top of the cake with apricot glaze and cover with the remaining pieces of almond paste. Roll lightly with a sugar-dusted rolling pin: make sure the joins adhere well. If you run a straight-sided jam jar round the cake this will smooth the paste and help it to adhere firmly to the cake.

How to apply royal icing

Put on the first coat seven days before the cake is required.
1 To flat ice a cake: Keep the bowl of icing covered during use. It is wiser to apply the top and sides on separate days, though which you do first is a matter of personal choice. Put a little royal icing on the cake board and fix the cake in position. Place the board on an icing turntable.
2 The top: Place a quantity of royal icing in the centre of the cake. Spread it over the surface with a palette knife using a 'paddling' movement. Roughly remove surplus icing. Draw an icing ruler held at an angle of about 30° with the cake top, and with a straight, firm movement draw it towards you, taking care to press evenly and not too heavily. Repeat until surface is smooth, adding more icing if necessary. Holding the blade of a clean palette knife parallel with the side of the cake, remove surplus icing from top edge.
3 The sides: Coat these the next day, when the top is dry. Cover the sides with icing as for the top, using a paddling motion. Hold a plain-edged scraper or a small palette knife in one hand to the side of the cake and at a slight angle towards it. Pass the other hand under and around the turntable so that a little more than a complete revolution can be made. Keeping the scraper quite still in the right hand, revolve the turntable with the left hand smoothly and fairly quickly. Towards the end of the revolution draw the scraper away, to produce little if any take-off mark. Remove any surplus icing over the edge by means of a knife.
4 Second coat: To achieve a professional finish, apply a second coat of slightly thinner icing, preferably 48 hours after the first one. Trim off any rough protruding icing with a sharp knife or fine sandpaper, to give a smooth finish, before you apply the second coat in two stages as before. The exposed part of the cake board can also be 'flooded' with thinned icing. Remove surplus from edges and clean the rim. Leave to dry.

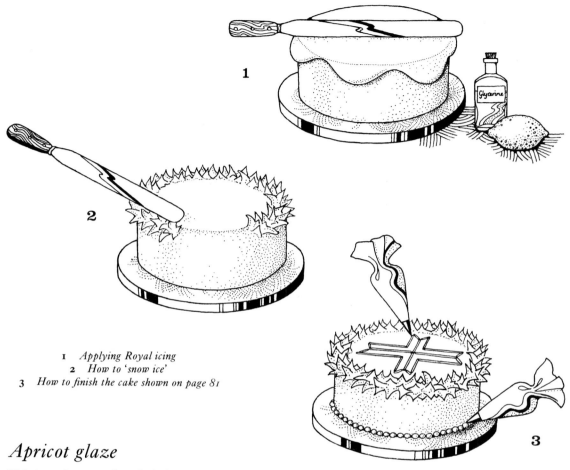

1   *Applying Royal icing*
2   *How to 'snow ice'*
3   *How to finish the cake shown on page 81*

Apricot glaze

This is used to coat the cake before the almond paste is applied.

Place 225 g (8 oz) apricot jam and 30 ml (2 tbsp) water in a saucepan over a low heat and stir until the jam softens. Sieve the mixture, return it to the pan and bring to the boil, boiling gently until the glaze is of a suitable coating consistency. This glaze can be stored and sealed in jars as for jam and kept for future use.

Almond paste

This makes 450 g (1 lb) paste.

100 g (4 oz) icing sugar, sifted
100 g (4 oz) caster sugar
225 g (8 oz) ground almonds
5 ml (1 tsp) lemon juice
almond essence
beaten egg to mix

Blend together the sugars and ground almonds, add the lemon juice, a few drops of almond essence and enough beaten egg to bind the mixture together to give a firm but manageable dough. Turn it out on to a sugared surface and knead lightly until smooth.

Royal icing

This recipe makes 900 g (2 lb) of icing. Dried egg albumen can be used instead of egg white – follow recommended instructions carefully.

4 egg whites
900 g (2 lb) icing sugar, sifted
15 ml (1 tbsp) lemon juice
10 ml (2 tsp) glycerine

Whisk the egg whites in a bowl until slightly frothy. Stir in the sugar, a spoonful at a time, with a wooden spoon. When half the sugar is incorporated, add the lemon juice. Continue adding more sugar, beating well after each addition until you get the right consistency – the mixture is right for coating when it is slightly softer than the peak stage when pulled up with a wooden spoon; it should be a little stiffer for piping purposes. Lastly, stir in the glycerine, which helps prevent the icing from becoming too hard. If you use an electric mixer, take care not to over-beat, for if royal icing becomes too fluffy, it gives a rough surface and breaks when piped. It's a good idea to let the icing stand for 24 hours in a covered plastic container.

For a special 'snow scene' effect, apply more icing in a thicker layer to the sides of the cake, and extend it in a 2.5-cm (1-in) border round the edge of the flat top. Level it roughly, then quickly flick it up into peaks, using a round-bladed knife or the handle of a teaspoon (*see photograph on page 81*).

A quick and effective finish for the sides of a cake coated with royal icing (or with butter cream or creme au beurre), is to 'rib' it. Over the flat-icing apply a second coat of royal icing and level roughly. Holding an icing comb at an angle of 45°, draw it over the sides to give a ridged effect. Keep your fingers well splayed over the comb to give an even pressure.

All about piping

There are various kinds of icing suitable for piping decoration on cakes: butter cream, crème au beurre, stiff glacé icing and royal icing can all be used successfully. Butter cream or glacé icing should be used for decorating sponge cakes, and royal icing for the formal decoration of fruit cakes. When you are decorating a royal-iced cake, let the flat coat of icing harden for about two days before applying the piping. The icing must be free of all lumps which might block the piping nozzle and must also be of a consistency that it can be 'forced' easily through the nozzle while retaining its shape without strong pressure.

HOW TO MAKE A FORCING BAG

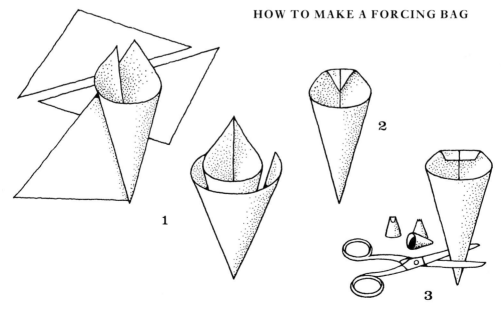

1   *Fold a 25 cm (10 in) square of greaseproof paper into a triangle. Roll it up along the longest edge, so that it looks like an ice cream cone*
2   *Fold over the top to secure the seam*
3   *Snip off the tip of the bag and insert nozzle if being used*

To make a forcing bag

Fold a 25-cm (10-in) square of greaseproof paper into a triangle, and then fold as in diagram. It's a good idea to secure the folded top with a staple.

Cut a small piece off the tip of the bag and drop in the required metal nozzle.

To use the bag, place a little icing in it and fold the top over once or twice, pressing the icing down to the tip of the nozzle. It is important not to over-fill the bag as this makes it more difficult to handle. When piping, hold the bag in one hand as though it were a pencil, with the thumb on top to give an even pressure. If you are inexperienced, first practice piping on an upturned plate. Icing can be removed while it is still soft, so mistakes can be corrected.

The nozzles

For a simple design – which is often the most effective – these types of nozzles are usually needed:
1 Plain nozzles in three sizes, to make lines, scallops, dots and words.
2 A star nozzle for rosettes, zigzags and ropes.
3 A shell nozzle.
If you are using a home made piping bag, buy nozzles without a screw-band. Screw bands are used to make a close fit with the screw collars to be found on shop-bought icing bags.

Piping techniques

To pipe lines Use a writing nozzle. Make contact with the iced surface and squeeze out just enough icing to stick to the surface. Continue squeezing and at the same time raise the bag and pull it gently towards you; hold the bag at an angle of about 45°. Lift the nozzle and line of piped icing from the surface, to keep a sagging line. The icing can then be guided and lowered into the required design.

To pipe stars and scrolls Use a star nozzle. For **stars**, hold the nozzle almost upright to the iced surface, the top of the nozzle almost on the surface. Pipe out a little icing, then withdraw the nozzle with a quick but hardly noticeable down-and-up action. For **scrolls**, hold the bag as for a straight line. With the nozzle almost on the iced surface, pipe out a good 'head', then gradually release the pressure and pull away with a double or single curve; the whole operation is done continuously. For a **twisted scroll**, pipe as for a straight line, but coil the icing so that each coil falls back against the previous one. The twisted scroll can be graduated from narrow, through wide to narrow again.

For tiered cakes the design is quite often continued from tier to tier by graduating the size of the nozzles, large ones being used, for example, on the base, and smaller nozzles for the upper tiers.

Border designs Bold patterns such as shells, ropes and rosettes are used where cake and board meet; delicate lines and dots are used for the sides and top.

Trellis This can be very effective. Using a writing nozzle, pipe parallel lines in one direction across the space to be covered; when these are dry, pipe more lines on top of them, but in the other direction. For a really good finish, pipe another line on top of the second set, using a very fine pipe. If any 'tails' of icing are left at beginning and end of a line, trim them off while still soft. Don't attempt to pipe a line with the nozzle touching the cake, as this results in an uneven finish – hold the top of the nozzle above the surface of the cake and let the icing fall in a straight line.

Run-outs These can either be piped directly on to the cake, or on to waxed paper and attached when dry to the cake as a relief design. Lettering and simple traced or free-hand drawn outlines of bells, leaves, candles, plaques and so on, are all suitable. Draw the outline distinctly on a piece of white card. Cut waxed paper to cover amply. Place a piece over the outline and fix with a spot of icing at each corner. Trace with a fine or medium writing nozzle. Thin down the icing to a 'just-flowing' consistency with unwhisked egg white. Pour it into a paper forcing-bag, then cut the tip off the bag and pipe the icing into the outlined shape. If the icing is the correct consistency, it will fall smoothly into place. Leave on a flat surface to dry for several days. Peel off the paper.

Christmas cake

COLOUR PLATE PAGE 81

225 g (8 oz) plain flour
2.5 ml (½ level tsp) ground ginger
2.5 ml (½ level tsp) ground mace
225 g (8 oz) butter
225 g (8 oz) dark, soft brown sugar
4 large eggs, beaten
grated rind of 1 lemon
225 g (8 oz) currants, cleaned
225 g (8 oz) stoned raisins, cleaned and
    roughly chopped
225 g (8 oz) sultanas, cleaned
100 g (4 oz) small glacé cherries, halved
100 g (4 oz) mixed chopped peel
50 g (2 oz) almonds, chopped
15–30 ml (1–2 tbsp) brandy

Line a 20.5 cm (8-in) round cake tin (*see page 115*). Sift the flour with the spices. Cream the butter and sugar together in a bowl with a wooden spoon; beat well until the mixture is pale in colour, light and fluffy in texture, and about twice its original volume. Add 15 ml (1 tbsp) egg at a time to the creamed mixture, beating well. If the mixture shows signs of curdling, beat in 15–30 ml (1–2 level tbsp) of the sifted flour. Lightly fold or beat in the remaining flour, alternately with the lemon rind, fruit and nuts. Mix thoroughly to distribute the fruit evenly.

Add the brandy and mix in. Then spoon all the mixture into the prepared tin.

With the back of a spoon, hollow the centre of the mixture, to prevent uneven rising. Bake in the oven at 150°C (300°F) mark 1–2, for about $3\frac{3}{4}$ hours. If the cake shows signs of browning up too quickly, cover with a sheet of greaseproof paper and reduce the heat to 140°C (275°F) mark $\frac{1}{2}$ for the last hour or so of the time. Cool in tin for at least an hour, turn on to wire rack.

Light Christmas cake

175 g (6 oz) glacé cherries, halved
175 g (6 oz) currants
175 g (6 oz) sultanas
100 g (4 oz) glacé pineapple
100 g (4 oz) chopped mixed peel
225 g (8 oz) butter or block margarine
225 g (8 oz) caster sugar
50 g (2 oz) ground almonds
4 eggs, beaten
225 g (8 oz) self-raising flour
grated rind and juice of 1 lemon
45 ml (3 tbsp) brandy

Line a 23-cm (9-in) cake tin, using a double thickness of greaseproof paper. If the cherries are very syrupy, wash them and dry well. Clean the currants and sultanas if necessary. Cut the glacé pineapple into small pieces.

Cream the fat and sugar until pale and fluffy and stir in the ground almonds. Add the eggs a little at a time, beating well after each addition. Add 45 ml (3 level tbsp) of the flour to the fruits and peel, mixing well. Fold these ingredients alternately with the rest of the flour, the grated lemon rind and the lemon juice, into the creamed mixture. Lastly, stir in the brandy. Put the mixture into the tin and bake in the oven at 170°C (325°F) mark 3, for about $2\frac{1}{2}$ hours, or until risen and just firm to the touch. Cool on a wire rack.

White fruit cake

This makes a good alternative to the traditional Christmas cake, appropriately iced and decorated.

100 g (4 oz) plain flour
100 g (4 oz) self-raising flour
50 g (2 oz) cornflour
100 g (4 oz) glacé pineapple
175 g (6 oz) glacé cherries
100 g (4 oz) mixed glacé fruits
50 g (2 oz) crystallised ginger
50 g (2 oz) chopped mixed peel
50 g (2 oz) angelica
50 g (2 oz) blanched almonds
50 g (2 oz) shelled walnuts
225 g (8 oz) butter or block margarine
150 g (5 oz) caster sugar
4 large eggs
15 ml (1 tbsp) lemon juice
45–60 ml (3–4 tbsp) milk

Line a 20.5-cm (8-in) round cake tin (*see page 115*). Sift together the flours and cornflour. Cut the fruit into pieces about the size of half a cherry. Trim the angelica into matchsticks. Chop the nuts roughly. Mix the fruits and nuts together. Dust 30 ml (2 level tbsp) flour over all to coat the sticky fruit. Cream together the fat and sugar, slowly beat in the eggs one at a time, with a little flour. Lightly beat in the remaining flour with the lemon juice and milk. Fold in the fruit and nuts. Turn the mixture into the prepared tin, hollow the centre and bake in the oven at 170°C (325°F) mark 3, for 2–$2\frac{1}{2}$ hours. Leave in the tin for 15 minutes, turn out then cool on a wire rack.

Ingredients used in cake making

Raising agents

Every cook wants her cakes and bakes to 'rise' perfectly. The rising or raising process is achieved by introducing air, carbon dioxide or steam into the mixture and trapping it there. This is done by hand (during the creaming process in cakes, for example, and by folding and rolling of flaky or puff pastry) and by incorporating one or more of the following raising agents into the mixture.

Baking powder is the most commonly used chemical raising agent. It consists of bicarbonate of soda and an acid-reacting chemical such as cream of tartar. With moisture and heat these react together to produce the gas carbon dioxide. When wet, the gluten in the flour is capable of holding the gas made by the raising agent in the form of tiny bubbles. These bubbles become larger during baking and thus the cake rises. The heat dries and sets the gluten and so the bubbles are held, giving the cake its characteristic texture. However, cake mixtures are capable of holding only a certain amount of gas, and if too much raising agent is used the cake rises very well at first, but then collapses, and a heavy, close texture is the final result.

A combination of **bicarbonate of soda** and **cream of tartar** is sometimes used to replace baking powder. Sour milk is used in some cakes and scones; as it contains an acid, the amount of cream of tartar should be reduced.

Yeast, *see page 12.*

Eggs help the raising process in three ways. First, the whisking of eggs produces thousands of tiny air bubbles which are then incorporated into the mixture (the egg white whisked alone is more effective than the whole egg – the egg yolk decreases the foaming action). Second, the mixture contained in the egg produces steam during cooking. Third, as the mixture cooks the protein in egg yolk coagulates or 'sets' thus holding the trapped air in suspension. In creamed mixtures also the eggs are beaten in and – so long as the correct proportion of egg is used and the mixture is well beaten – little additional raising agent is required. In plain cakes, where beaten egg is added together with the liquid, the egg helps to bind the mixture, but it does not act as the main raising agent.

Flour

As we explained in the breadmaking chapter, there are two main types of flour available: strong flour made from hard wheat, which has a high gluten content of 10–15 per cent; and soft flour milled from soft wheat with a lower gluten content of 7–10 per cent. Strong flour has the high raising, water absorbing qualities which give the large volume and light open texture to bread and other recipes using yeast. Soft flour is best for cakes and pastries where a smaller rise and a closer, finer texture is required.

By varying the other ingredients used with flour, the gluten can be toughened or softened to produce the right kind of mixture. Soft flours will absorb fat well to produce a light, soft texture. A soft flour can be plain or self-raising. Many cakes are made with self-raising flour. This is popular because it eliminates errors as the raising agents are evenly blended throughout the flour. A mixture of both plain and self-raising is best for some rich cakes where the amount of raising agent would be too great if only self-raising flour were used. Alternatively, plain flour can be used with the necessary quantity of raising agent added to suit the recipe (the amount needed will be indicated in the recipe). If you only have a plain flour, add 12.5 ml (2½ level tsp) baking powder to 225 g (8 oz) of the plain flour to replace the same quantity of self-raising flour. Sift flour and baking powder together two or three times to mix thoroughly before use.

Sugar

Sugar is an important ingredient in cake baking. Brown sugars and other kinds can give variety and extra flavour if correctly used.

Caster sugar is the one most commonly used in cake recipes. It is the best for creamed mixtures and whisked sponge mixtures.

Granulated sugar produces a creamed mixture which is slighly reduced in volume, with a reasonably good texture, apart from a slight grittiness and sometimes a speckly appearance. For rubbed-in mixtures, granulated sugar is quite acceptable.

Icing sugar is the finest textured sugar. It is not generally used for basic cake mixtures, as the volume produced is poor and the crust hard, but it is favoured for some biscuit and meringue recipes. It is ideal for decorating cakes, and for icing mixtures.

Soft brown sugar whether dark or light, imparts more flavour – a caramel taste – than white sugar and has a slightly finer grain. When it is used to replace caster sugar in sandwich cakes, the volume is just as good. Soft brown sugars also cream well.

Demerara sugar is coarser in grain than granulated, which it can replace in rubbed-in mixtures. It is more suitable for making cakes by the melting method, such as gingerbreads, where heat and moisture help to dissolve it. It is unsatisfactory for creamed mixtures, because its large crystals do not break down during the mixing.

Barbados sugar is a very dark, treacle-coloured unrefined sugar. It is too strong in flavour for light cake mixtures, but helps give a good flavour and colour to rich fruit cakes and to gingerbreads.

Other sweeteners

Golden syrup Can be used to replace part of the sugar content in a recipe.

Treacle, a dark syrup, is not as sweet as golden syrup. A little added to rich fruit cakes gives a good dark colour and distinctive flavour; it is also a traditional ingredient for gingerbreads and for the making of malt bread.

Honey absorbs and retains moisture, and this helps prevent cakes drying out and going stale. Only part of the sugar content should be replaced by honey – generally not more than half.

Fats

The commonest fats used in baking are butter and margarine, but others, such as lard and oil may be used. Butter and block margarine are interchangeable, though butter gives a better flavour. Soft tub margarines are suited to special all-in-one recipes. Oil is often used today, but specially proportioned recipes are needed (*see pages 59 and 60*).

Eggs

As already explained, the inclusion of eggs in a whisked or creamed cake mixture makes use of air as a raising agent instead of carbon dioxide. If an extra light mixture is required, the egg whites are whisked separately before being added.

For baking purposes eggs should be used at room temperature. A standard egg weighing roughly 50 g (2 oz) is a suitable size for most recipes and standard eggs have been used throughout the book except where stated otherwise (for example where eggs are used as the raising agent and a larger volume is required, eg whisked sponge).

Liquid

Moisture is required for the evolution of steam. Generally, the liquid in a mixture is milk or water. Sour milk and buttermilk improve the taste of certain kinds of bread and scones.

Cake making methods

Creamed method

This method forms the basis of many cakes from the classic Victoria Sandwich to rich fruit cakes.

1 Use a bowl size appropriate for the quantity of the mixture. A deep bowl is best when using a hand mixer.
2 Cream the fat with the sugar until light and fluffy. This incorporates air and increases the volume of the mixture. When the fat is hard it is easier to cut it into pieces; place in a warm bowl and beat before adding the sugar.
3 Beat in the eggs gradually.
4 Fold or beat in the flour by hand.
5 Fold in any additional ingredients such as dried fruit etc.

One-stage method

This is a wonderfully quick and simple method to make a cake without rubbing in or creaming the fat first – but it's best to use a soft tub margarine.

1 Place all the ingredients together in a bowl.
2 Mix very thoroughly, scraping round the sides of the bowl to incorporate all the mixture.
3 Take care not to over-beat, particularly if you are using an electric mixer, as this will give you a heavy-textured cake.

Melted method

This quick, easy method is best for cakes that use baking powder and bicarbonate of soda as the raising agents, for example gingerbread. The texture of cakes made by this method is often fairly sticky, but this varies according to the richness of the mixture.

1 Sift all the dry ingredients into a bowl.
2 Melt the fat with the sugar or syrup and allow to cool slightly.

3 Stir the melted fat and other liquid into the dry ingredients.

Whisked sponge method

Whisked sponges are the lightest of all cake mixtures. They contain no raising agent and rely solely on the incorporation of air to raise the mixture.

1 Whisk the eggs and sugar together in a deep bowl over a saucepan of hot (not boiling) water until thick and creamy. When lifted from the mixture the whisk should leave a trail for a few seconds. (If you are using an electric mixer, no heat is required during whisking.)
2 Remove from the heat. Cool.
3 Sift the flour over the surface and, using a metal spoon, gently incorporate the flour into the mixture in a figure of eight motion.

Alternative method

1 Separate the eggs, whisk the yolks with the sugar over the heat.
2 Fold in the flour.
3 Whisk the whites separately and fold into the mixture.

Rubbed in method

This is the simplest method for making plain cakes. Cakes made using this method are generally best eaten fresh or within a day or two of being made.

1 Sift the flour into a bowl, add fat, cut in small pieces.
2 Rub in the fat (usually in the proportion of half fat to flour) carefully with the fingertips to ensure that it is evenly distributed throughout.
3 Add the egg(s) and enough liquid to bind the mixture and make it of a soft dropping consistency.

Preparing cake tins

Greasing
Grease all cake tins lightly with melted fat or oil. The quickest method is to brush them over with a pastry brush dipped in the melted fat or oil. As an additional precaution against sticking sprinkle a little flour in the greased tin and shake until coated, then tip out any surplus.

For sponge cakes, first grease the tins, then dust them with 5 ml (1 level tsp) flour mixed with 5 ml (1 level tsp) caster sugar.

Lining

Use greaseproof paper to line tins and grease the paper before putting in the mixture. Alternatively, use a non-stick paper, which can be used several times and does not require greasing. For Victoria sandwiches, line the bottoms of the tins with a round of greaseproof paper; for rich mixtures and fruit cakes, line the whole tin (see below).

Cake tins with a non-stick finish do not require greasing or lining, but be sure to follow the manufacturer's directions regarding their use and general care.

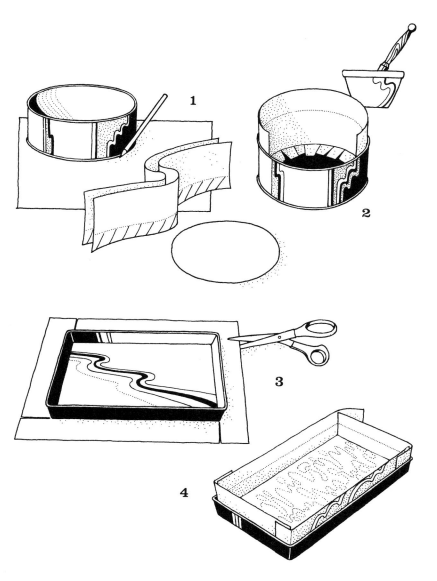

HOW TO LINE A CAKE TIN

1 *Measure around the base of the tin. Slash paper for the sides at 2.5 cm (1 in) intervals*
2 *Fit the paper into the sides of the tins*
3 *For square cornered tins cut out paper 5 cm (2 in) larger than the tin.*
Cut each corner of the paper as far as the tin
4 *Place the paper in the tin so that it fits closely, overlapping at the corners*

To line a deep tin Cut a piece of greaseproof paper long enough to reach round the tin and high enough to extend about 5 cm (2 in) above the top edge. Cut another piece to fit the bottom of the tin. Fold up the bottom edge of the long strip about 2.5 cm (1 in), creasing it firmly, and snip this folded portion with a pair of scissors; this enables the paper band to fit a square or round tin neatly. Brush both pieces of paper with melted fat and place the strip in position first: the bottom piece keeps the snipped edge of the band in position and makes a neat lining.

Extra protection for rich mixtures: wrap a double thickness of brown paper round the outside and secure with string. Place tin on double thickness of brown paper.

To line a sandwich tin Cut a round of greaseproof paper to fit the bottom of the greased tin exactly. To give a straight-sided shallow tin extra depth, line the sides also, letting the side strip project 2.5 cm (1 in) above the rim.

To line a Swiss roll tin Cut a piece of paper about 5 cm (2 in) larger all round than the tin. Place the tin on it and in each corner make a cut from the corner of the paper as far as the corner of the tin. Grease both paper and tin and put in the paper so that it fits closely, overlapping at the corners.

Juggling with tins
If you don't possess the right size tin for the recipe, or you wish to use a fancy shaped tin instead, you will need to know how much mixture to make. This depends on knowing the volume of *liquid* the tin will hold. The following chart shows the liquid capacity in 600 ml (pints) of both round and square tins. The figures are based on an average finished cake depth of 7.5 cm (3 in) and the capacities are worked out to the nearest 300 ml ($\frac{1}{2}$ pint). The first set of figures in each column are in metric measurements (as indicated), the second set (in brackets) are the equivalent imperial measurements.

Chart showing liquid capacity of cake tins

Round tin: Size in cm	(in)	Capacity in ml (pints)		Square tin: size in cm	(in)	Capacity in litres (pints)	
12.5	(5)	600	(1)	12.5	(5)	1.1	(2)
15	(6)	900	(1½)	15	(6)	1.4	(2½)
18	(7)	1.1 l	(2)	18	(7)	1.7	(3)
20.5	(8)	1.7 l	(3)	20.5	(8)	2.3	(4)
23	(9)	2.3 l	(4)	23	(9)	3.4	(6)
25.5	(10)	3.4 l	(6)	25.5	(10)	4.5	(8)
28	(11)	4.5 l	(8)	28	(11)	5.7	(10)
30.5	(12)	5.7 l	(10)	30.5	(12)	6.8	(12)
33	(13)	6.8 l	(12)	33	(13)	8	(14)
35.5	(14)	9 l	(16)	35.5	(14)	9	(16)

Cake baking know-how

Before starting, make sure that the oven will be at the correct temperature by the time it is required. Temperatures are given in each recipe. Use the oven positions recommended by the manufacturer.

Testing whether a cake is cooked
Small cakes should be well risen, golden brown in colour and just firm to the touch and they should begin to shrink from the sides of the tin on being taken out of the oven.

Larger cakes present more difficulty, especially for beginners. The oven heat and time of cooking give a reasonable indication, but the following tests are helpful:

1 For light mixtures press the centre top of the cake very lightly with the finger-tip. The cake should be spongy and should give only very slightly to the pressure. When the finger-tip is removed, the surface should rise again immediately, retaining no impression.

2 If you're baking a fruit cake, lift it gently from the oven and 'listen' to it, putting it closely to the ear. A continued sizzling sound indicates that the cake is not cooked through.

3 Insert a fine skewer or metal knitting needle (never a cold knife) in the centre of the cake. It should come out perfectly clean. If any mixture is sticking to it, the cake requires more cooking.

HOW TO TEST WHETHER A SPONGE CAKE IS COOKED AND HOW TO TURN OUT OF TIN

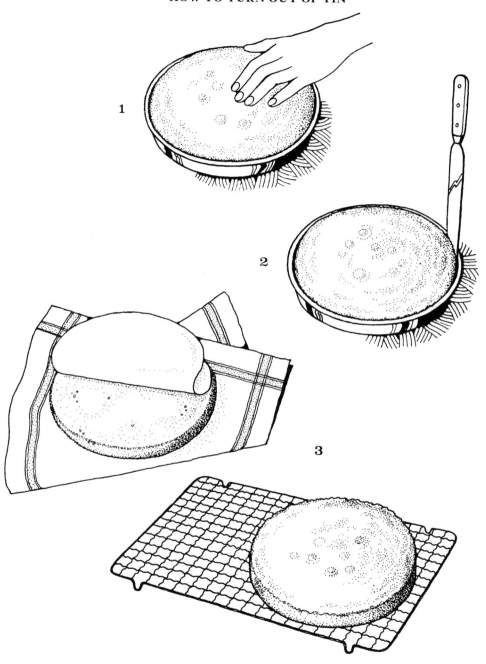

1   *Press cake lightly with fingertips. If cooked, a sponge cake should be just firm*
to the touch and spring back when lightly pressed
2   *Ease the cake from the sides of the tin with a round bladed knife, if necessary*
3   *Turn the cake out of the tin on to a clean towel or oven glove. Remove the paper from the base.*
Quickly invert on to cooling rack top side up

Cooling

Allow the cake a few minutes or more as instructed to cool before turning it out of the tin; during this time it will shrink away from the sides and so be more easily removed. If necessary ease from the sides with a round bladed knife. Turn it out very gently, remove any paper and place, right side up, on a wire rack.

Storing

When the cake is completely cold put it in a tin with a tightly fitting lid.

Most types of cake are best eaten quite fresh, but rich fruit cakes and gingergreads improve with keeping and should be stored for at least 24 hours before being cut – even longer if they are really rich. Fruit cakes which are to be kept for any length of time should be wrapped in greaseproof paper or foil before being put in the tin.

Un-iced cakes can be stored by wrapping them first in greaseproof paper and then in foil or self-sealing plastic film. This is especially useful for awkward-sized cakes. Iced cakes are best stored in a tin, but can be very loosely 'capped' with foil, so that the icing is not disturbed.

After a wedding cake has been decorated it should be lightly covered with paper and allowed to dry overnight. It should then be completely covered with cling film and sealed to exclude all dust, and should remain covered until required. White cakes show every mark, and there is no way of removing dust

from icing. As royal icing tends to become hard when kept, a cake should not be decorated too long before it is required.

Biscuits and cookies should also be stored in a tightly closed tin or container. Each variety should be stored separately. Never store cakes and biscuits in the same tin, or the biscuits will absorb moisture from the cakes and lose their crispness. Most iced biscuits are best eaten fresh.

Freezing

Most undecorated cakes – sponge, creamed Victoria, Madeira, light fruit cakes and small buns – will freeze well. Wrap them in freezer wrapping, then seal with freezer tape, excluding as much air as possible. Frosted and iced cakes are only suitable for short-term storage. Don't fill sponges with jam before freezing, as this tends to make them soggy. It is a good idea to freeze the parts for a filled cake separately, putting together, for example, the sandwich layers, cream rosettes and strawberries while they are still frozen and allowing the cake to thaw out before serving.

When freezing a glacé-iced or butter-cream frosted gâteau, put it in the freezer without wrapping until it is firm, then wrap. To prevent crushing, the cake may be placed in a heavy cardboard box. Pack cup cakes in a single layer in a rigid box, then overwrap. See the following chart for recommended storage time.

BASIC FREEZER KNOW-HOW

Food and storage time	Preparation	Freezing	Thawing and serving
BISCUITS *baked and unbaked* 6 months	Prepare in the usual way. Iced biscuits do not freeze well.	Either baked or unbaked, pack carefully. Wrap rolls of uncooked dough, or pipe soft mixtures into shapes, open freeze and pack when firm. Allow cooked biscuits to cool before packing.	Thaw uncooked rolls of dough slightly; slice off required number of biscuits and bake. Shaped biscuits can be cooked direct from frozen state: allow 7–10 minutes extra cooking time. Cooked biscuits may require crisping in a warm oven.
BREAD 4 weeks	Freshly-baked bread, both home-made and bought, can be frozen. Crisp, crusty bread stores well up to 1 week, then the crust begins to 'shell off'.	Home-made bread: freeze in foil or freezer bags. Bought bread: in original wrapper for up to 1 week; for longer periods, seal in foil or freezer bags.	Leave to thaw in the sealed bag at room temperature for 3–6 hours, or overnight in the refrigerator, or leave foil-wrapped and crisp in the oven at 200°C (400°F) mark 6, for about 45 minutes. Sliced bought bread can be toasted from its frozen state.

Food and storage time	Preparation	Freezing	Thawing and serving
SCONES AND TEABREADS 6 months	Bake in usual way.	Freeze in freezer bags in convenient units for serving.	Thaw teabreads in wrapping at room temperature for 2–3 hours. Scones: reheat from frozen, wrapped in foil, at 200°C (400°F) mark 6, for 10 minutes. Griddle scones: thaw 1 hour. Drop scones: thaw 30 minutes or cover and reheat for 10 minutes.
CROISSANTS AND DANISH PASTRIES *Unbaked in bulk:* 6 weeks *Baked:* 4 weeks	Unbaked: prepare to the stage at which all the fat has been absorbed, but don't give the final rolling. Baked: bake in usual way.	Unbaked and baked: wrap in airtight freezer bags and freeze at once.	Leave unbaked dough in bag, but unseal and re-tie loosely, allowing space for dough to rise. Preferably thaw overnight in a refrigerator, or leave for 5 hours at room temperature. Complete the final rolling and shaping, and bake.
CAKES *cooked* including sponge flans, Swiss rolls and layer cakes: 6 months *Frosted cakes:* 2 months	Bake in usual way. Leave until cold on a wire rack. Swiss rolls are best rolled up in cornflour, not sugar, if they are to be frozen without a filling. Do not spread or layer with jam before freezing. Keep essences to a minimum and go lightly on the spices.	Wrap plain cake layers separately, or together with Saran or waxed paper between layers. Freeze frosted cakes (whole or cut) unwrapped until frosting has set, then wrap, seal and pack in boxes to protect icing.	Iced cakes: unwrap before thawing, then the wrapping will not stick to the frosting when thawing. Cream cakes: may be sliced while frozen for a better shape and quick thawing. Plain cakes: leave in package and thaw at room temperature. Un-iced layer cakes and small cakes thaw in about 1–2 hours at room temperature: frosted layer cakes take up to 4 hours.
CAKE MIXTURES *uncooked* 2 months	Whisked sponge mixtures do not freeze well uncooked. Put rich creamed mixtures into containers, or line the tin to be used later with greased foil and add cake mixture.	Freeze uncovered. When frozen, remove from tin, package in foil and overwrap. Return to freezer.	To thaw, leave at room temperature for 2–3 hours, then fill tins to bake. Pre-formed cake mixtures can be returned to the original tin, without wrapping but still in foil lining. Place frozen in pre-heated oven and bake in usual way, but allow longer cooking time.
PASTRY *uncooked* *Shortcrust:* 3 months *Flaky and puff:* 3–4 months *Note* there is little advantage in bulk-freezing short-crust pastry, as it takes about 3 hours to thaw before it can be rolled out. For bulk-freezing flaky and puff pastry – prepare up to the last rolling; pack in freezer bags or heavy-duty foil and overwrap. To use, leave for 3–4 hours at room temperature, or overnight in refrigerator.	Roll out to size required. Freeze pie shells unwrapped until hard, to avoid damage. Discs of pastry can be stacked with wax paper between for pie bases or tops.	Stack pastry shapes with two pieces of Saran or waxed paper between layers, so that if needed, one piece of pastry can be removed without thawing the whole batch. Place the stack on a piece of cardboard, wrap and seal.	Thaw flat discs at room temperature, fit into pie plate and proceed with recipe. Unbaked pie shells or flat cases should be returned to their original container before cooking: they can go into the oven from the freezer (oven-proof glass should first stand for 10 minutes at room temperature); add about 5 minutes to normal baking time.

Food and storage time	Preparation	Freezing	Thawing and serving
PASTRY *cooked* *Pastry cases:* 6 months	Prepare as usual. Empty cases freeze satisfactorily, but with some change in texture.	Wrap carefully – very fragile.	Flan cases should be thawed at room temperature for about 1 hour; refresh if wished.
CREAM *Whipped:* 3 months *Commercially frozen:* up to 1 year	Use only pasteurised, with a 40% butter-fat content or more (i.e. double cream). Best results are achieved with half-whipped cream with 5 ml (1 level tsp) caster sugar to 142 ml (¼ pint). Whipped cream may be piped into rosettes on waxed paper for freezing.	Transfer cream to suitable container, eg waxed carton, leaving space for expansion. Freeze rosettes unwrapped; when firm, pack in a single layer in foil.	Thaw in refrigerator, allowing 24 hours, or 12 hours at room temperature. Put rosettes in position as decoration before thawing, as they cannot be handled once thawed. Rosettes take a shorter time to thaw.

Tricks of the trade

To clean fruit
Fruit should be picked over and cleaned before use, unless the cleaned packaged kind is bought. To clean currants, sultanas and raisins, wash them in cold water and drain; dry in a cloth, then spread out on a flat tin or sieve and dry off very slowly in a warm place. For quick cleaning, rub them on a wire sieve or in a tea towel with a little flour, then pick over to remove any stalks. Discard surplus flour.

To shred peel
Remove the sugar and cut the peel into fine shreds or chop with a very sharp knife. If the peel is very hard, soak it for a minute or two in boiling water, then dry and cut it up. Ready cut (chopped) mixed peel tends to be rather coarsely cut. Further chopping is often needed.

To separate an egg
Give the egg a sharp knock against the side of a basin or cup and break the shell in half – tapping it lightly two or three times is liable to crush the shell instead of breaking it cleanly and may cause the yolk to mix into the white. Having broken the shell, pass the yolk back and forth from one half of the shell to the other, letting the white drop into the basin. Put the yolk into another basin.

If you are separating more than one egg, use a third basin for cracking the eggs (so that if any of the yolk should break, only the one white will be spoilt); put the second yolk in with the first one and tip the white in the first white. Continue using the third basin in this way for any more eggs that may be needed.

To blanch almonds
Put in a saucepan with cold water to cover, bring just to the boil, strain and run cold water over them. Then rub between finger and thumb to remove the skins, which will slip off quite easily.

To sliver almonds
First blanch the nuts, then split each in half with a small, sharp-pointed knife. Place flat on a chopping board and, while the nuts are still damp, cut into long, thin strips.

To toast nuts, spread out in a shallow pan and brown lightly under a medium grill, turning them occasionally, or bake in a moderate oven 180°C (350°F) mark 4 for 10–12 minutes; watch them carefully. Commercially ready-chopped almonds are known as 'nibbed' almonds.

To skin hazelnuts
Heat them through in the oven or under a slow grill, shaking them occasionally to turn. Then rub them in a clean cloth or paper bag and the papery skins will crumble off.

To whip cream
Use double or whipping cream and chill it beforehand; place it in a chilled deep bowl and whisk with a cold rotary beater until it is fluffy and can just hold its shape. Be careful not to over-beat. (For less than 142 ml (¼ pint), it is safer to use a large fork or small balloon whisk.)

To make vanilla sugar
When buying vanilla pods, choose those covered with

white crystals, which indicate freshness. Label a jar with a good stopper or cover, fill with caster sugar and add a pod – the sugar will soon acquire the true vanilla flavour, and may be used to replace some of the sugar in a recipe. Remember that bought vanilla sugar is more strongly flavoured, so use it judiciously. Vanilla essence, too, is very concentrated; buy the best and use it sparingly.

To melt chocolate

Break the chocolate into pieces, put into a bowl and stand this over hot (*not* boiling) water. See that no water gets into the bowl and that the temperature of the chocolate does not become too high – chocolate melts at about 40°C (104°F). Remove the chocolate from the bowl with a scraper.

What went wrong?

CAKES

Too close a texture?
This may be caused by:

1 Too much liquid.
2 Too little raising agent.
3 Insufficient creaming of the fat and sugar – air should be well incorporated at this stage.
4 Curdling of the creamed mixture when the eggs are added (a curdled mixture holds less air than one of the correct texture).
5 Over-stirring or beating the flour into a creamed mixture when little or no raising agent is present.

Uneven texture with holes?
This may be caused by:

1 Over-stirring or uneven mixing in of the flour.
2 Putting the mixture into the cake tin in small amounts – pockets of air are trapped in the mixture.

Dry and crumbly texture?
This may be caused by:

1 Too much raising agent.
2 Too long a cooking time in too cool an oven.

'Peaking' and 'cracking'?
This may be caused by:

1 Too hot an oven.
2 The cake being placed too near top of the oven.
3 Too stiff a mixture.
4 Too small a cake tin.

Fruit cakes dry and crumbly?
This may be caused by:

1 Cooking at too high a temperature.
2 Too stiff a mixture.
3 Not lining the tin thoroughly – for a large cake, double greaseproof paper should be used.

Fruit sinking to the bottom of the cake?
This may be caused by:

1 Damp fruit. Though fruit needs cleaning, if it is washed it must be dried by being spread out on absorbent paper and left in a warm place to dry before use.
2 Sticky glacé cherries: if covered with thick syrup they should first be washed, then lightly floured.
3 Too soft a mixture: a rich fruit cake mixture should be fairly stiff, so that it can hold up the weight of the fruit.
4 Opening or banging the oven door while the cake is rising.
5 Using self-raising flour where the recipe requires plain, or using too much baking powder – the cake over-rises and cannot carry the fruit with it.

Cakes sinking in the middle?
This may be caused by:

1 Too soft a mixture.
2 Too much raising agent.
3 Too cool an oven, which means that the centre of the cake does not rise.
4 Too hot an oven, which makes the cake appear to be done on the outside before it is cooked through, so that it is taken from the oven too soon.
5 Too short a baking time.

Burnt fruit on the outside of a fruit cake?
This may be caused by:

1 Too high a temperature.
2 Lack of protection: as soon as the cake begins to colour, a piece of brown paper or a double thickness of greaseproof paper should be placed over the top for the remainder of the cooking time, to prevent further browning.

CAKES (*contd*)

Close, heavy-textured whisked sponge?
This may be caused by:

1 The eggs and sugar being insufficiently beaten, so that not enough air is enclosed.
2 The flour being stirred in too heavily or for too long – very light folding movements are required and a metal spoon should be used especially when plain flour and baking powder or entrapped air are used as the raising agent.

A heavy layer at the base of a Genoese sponge?
This may be caused by:

1 The melted fat being too hot – it should be only lukewarm and just flowing.
2 Uneven or insufficient folding in of fat or flour.
3 Pouring the fat into the centre of the mixture instead of round the edge.

SCONES

The scones are heavy and badly risen?
This may be caused by:

1 Insufficient raising agent.
2 Heavy handling, especially during the kneading.
3 Insufficient liquid.
4 Too cool an oven.

The scones have spread and lost their shape?
This may be caused by:
1 Slack dough, with too much liquid.
2 Too heavily greased a tin. The fat melts on heating in the oven and 'pulls out' the soft dough before it has set.
3 Careless kneading (especially of the scraps for the second rolling) or twisting the cutter round as the scones were stamped out.

They have a very rough surface when cooked?
This may be caused by:

1 Insufficient or careless kneading.
2 Rough handling as the scones were transferred from the board to the baking sheet.
3 Too stiff a dough.

They're under-cooked on top and black underneath?

This occurs if the baking sheet is too large for the oven and does not allow circulation of hot air – the heat hits the tray and is deflected down, causing over-cooking of the bottom of the scones and insufficient cooking of the top. There should be a gap of at least 5 cm (2 in) between the sides of the shelf and the baking sheet, especially over the flame in a gas oven.

GRIDDLE SCONES

Uneven cooking?
This may be due to using a frying pan with a thin, uneven base.

Spreading?
This happens if the batter is too thin; it should be so thick that it only just pours from the spoon.

Sticking?
The scones stick if the griddle was dirty or insufficiently greased. It should be 'seasoned' by being rubbed with salt (*see page 51*).

BREAD RECIPES

Bread is crumbly and goes stale quickly?
This may be caused by:

1 Too much yeast.
2 Too soft flour.
3 Rising too quickly in too warm a place – over-fermentation.

'Flying top' or cracked crust?
This may be caused by:

1 Too soft flour.
2 Too 'tight' a dough.
3 Insufficient fermentation.
4 Too much dough for size of tin.

BREAD RECIPES (*contd*)

Pale crust, flat top, poor volume?
This may be caused by:

1 Too wet or too dry dough.
2 Too little salt or yeast.
3 Too soft a flour, or self-raising type.
4 Proving at too high a temperature and/or too long.
5 Insufficiently kneaded dough.
6 Under-fermented dough.

Sour and yeasty flavour?
This may be caused by:

1 Too much yeast or stale yeast, or yeast creamed with sugar.
2 Too long fermentation.

Uneven texture and holes?
This may be caused by:

1 Too much liquid and/or salt.
2 Too long or too short fermentation.
3 Insufficient kneading after first rising.
4 Dough over-proved.
5 Dough left uncovered during rising, forming a hard skin which gives streaks when kneaded.

Heavy close texture?
This may be caused by:

1 Too soft flour.
2 Too much salt.
3 Insufficient kneading or fermentation time.
4 Leaving dough to rise in too hot a place, which kills the yeast.
5 Too cool an oven, resulting in too long a baking time.

A–Z of baking terms and basic methods

Baking Cooking in the oven by dry heat. This is the method of cooking used for most cakes, biscuits and pastries and for many other dishes.

Baking blind Baking flans, tarts and tartlets without a filling. To do this line the flan ring or pie dish with pastry and trim the edges. Cut a round of greased greaseproof paper or foil slightly larger than the pastry case, place it greased side down inside the pastry and half-fill it with raw haricot beans, rice or stale crusts of bread. Bake as directed in the recipe. Beans can be used again and again.

Beating Agitating an ingredient or a mixture by vigorously turning it over and over with an upward motion, in order to introduce air. A spoon, fork, whisk or electric mixer may be used.

Binding Adding a liquid, egg or melted fat to a dry mixture to hold it together.

Blanching (*see page 120*).

Blending Mixing flour, cornflour, rice flour and similar ground cereals to a smooth cream with a cold liquid (milk or water) before a boiling liquid is added. This is done to prevent lumps forming.

Brioche A light French yeast mixture, an enriched dough usually baked in deep fluted patty tins and finished with a knob of dough placed on the top.

Caramelising Cooking white sugar (granulated or caster) with very little or no water until it turns into a nut-brown syrup. Occasionally icing sugar is sprinkled heavily on the surface of, say, a gâteau and is caramelised by means of a hot skewer; this is known as branding.

Chopping Cutting food into very small pieces. The ingredient is placed on a chopping board and a very sharp knife is used with a quick up-and-down action.

Creaming The beating together of fat and sugar to resemble whipped cream in colour and texture, ie pale and fluffy. This method of mixing is used for cakes and puddings containing a high proportion of fat.

Curd The solid part of soured milk or junket.

Curdling The separating of fresh milk or sauce when acid is present and excessive heat applied. Also applied to creamed mixtures when the egg is beaten in too much at a time or cold from the refrigerator.

Dariole A small, narrow mould with sloping sides, used for setting creams and jellies and for baking or steaming puddings and small cakes.

Dough A thick mixture of uncooked flour and liquid, often combined with other ingredients. The term is not confined to yeast dough, but can include mixtures such as pastry, scones and biscuits.

Dredging Coating food heavily with a dry substance or mixture; especially flour and icing sugar, but also plain sugar of any type.

Dropping consistency The term used to describe the texture of a cake or pudding mixture before cooking. To test, fill a spoon with the mixture and hold it on its side above a basin – the mixture should drop off in 5 seconds without any movement of the spoon.

Dusting Sprinkling lightly with flour, sugar, spices or seasoning.

Folding in (sometimes called cutting and folding) Combining a whisked or creamed mixture with other ingredients so that it retains its lightness. This is a method used for certain cake mixtures and for meringues and soufflés. To fold in flour, sift it gently over the surface of the mixture and using a metal spoon, incorporate gently into the mixture using a figure of eight movement. The mixture must be folded very lightly and not be agitated more than absolutely necessary, because with every movement some of the air bubbles are broken down. This cannot be done with an electric mixer.

Genoese A sponge cake made of a whisked egg mixture enriched by the addition of melted butter. Also spelt 'Genoise'.

Girdle see griddle.

Glazing Applying a thin layer of syrup or jelly to the surface of a food so that the food is just coated, but the texture can still be seen. A mixture of beaten egg or milk brushed over scones or breads before baking to give a golden colour.

Griddle Flat, heavy, metal plate, usually with a hoop handle, for baking breads, scones, cakes on top of the cooker.

Grinding The process of reducing hard foodstuffs such as nuts and coffee beans to small particles by means of a food mill, or grinder.

Kneading The process used for combining a mixture (such as yeast dough or pastry) which is too stiff for stirring. Gather it into a ball and place on a board. If it is inclined to stick, first dust the board with flour; if the dough is of a soft type, flour the hands well. Pastry and scone doughs, etc., are kneaded lightly, the outside edges being brought into the centre of the mixture with the finger-tips. Bread dough, which

must be kneaded to distribute the yeast and gas evenly throughout the mixture, needs firmer treatment. The easiest way to deal with it is to pull out the dough with the right hand, then fold it back over itself and push it away with the ball or 'heel' of the hand; give a quarter-turn and repeat the process.

Knocking back (*see page 14*).

Leaven The ingredient which causes dough to rise, eg yeast, baking powder.

Meringue Egg white whisked until stiff, mixed with sugar and dried in a cool oven till crisp.

Mocha A blend of chocolate and coffee.

Moule à manqué A shallow, sloping-sided cake tin.

Pastry blender A device for 'cutting' cooking fats. It is particularly practical if the fat is a little on the soft side or the hands are warm.

Pastry wheel Small serrated wheel used for cutting pastry or biscuit mixtures, leaving a zigzag edge.

Piping Forcing cream or butter cream out of a piping bag through a nozzle, to decorate cakes, etc. Also used for cake mixtures and meringues. The bag may be made of cotton, nylon, plastic or greaseproof paper (*see page 109*).

Praline Flavoured with burnt almonds.

Proving (*see page 14*).

Pastry crimper Device used in a number of ways to give professional finish to a pie or flan edge and it is fine, too, for finishing a top coat of almond paste or marzipan as used on an Easter or Simnel cake.

Rice paper Edible paper made from the pitch of a Chinese tree, used when baking macaroon and other almond mixtures.

Rubbing in A method of incorporating fat into flour, used in making shortcrust pastry, plain cakes and biscuits, when a short texture is required (*see page 114*).

Sieving Rubbing or pressing food through a sieve; a wooden spoon is used to force it through.

Sifting Shaking a dry ingredient through a sieve or flour sifter, to remove lumps and aerate dry ingredients, or thoroughly blend two or more dry ingredients.

Straining Separating liquids from solids using a sieve, colander or muslin.

Syrup A concentrated solution of sugar in water,

used in making water ices, drinks and fruit dishes. Golden syrup is a by-product of sugar refining. Maple syrup is extracted from the N. American sugar maple.

Tepid Approximately blood heat, 43°C (110°F). Tepid water is obtained by adding 2 parts cold water to 1 part boiling water.

Tube pan Ring shaped tin for baking.

Turnovers Sweet or savoury pasties made by folding over a round or square of rolled out pastry into a semi-circle or triangle and baking on a flat baking sheet.

Vanilla sugar Sugar in which a vanilla pod has been left to infuse (*see page 120*).

Whisk A device made of hoops of metal in a rounded shape, used to incorporate air into a mixture.

Whisking Beating (*qv*) a substance, eg fresh cream, quickly, and steadily, in order to incorporate air thus increasing its volume and giving a lighter consistency.

Zest The coloured part of orange and lemon peel, containing the oil that gives the characteristic flavour. To obtain zest, remove the rind very thinly, with no pith, by grating or in slivers with a potato peeler. If it is required for a sweet dish, the zest can be rubbed off with a lump of sugar and the sugar incorporated into the recipe.

Index